SKILL SHARPENERS
Geography

3

Writing: Mike Graf
Editing: Lisa Vitarisi Mathews
Copy Editing: Cathy Harber
Art Direction: Yuki Meyer
Design/Production: Yuki Meyer
Jessica Onken

EMC 3743

Evan-Moor®

Visit
teaching-standards.com
to view a correlation
of this book.
This is a free service.

**Correlated to
Current Standards**

CPSIA: Asia Pacific Offset Ltd, Kowloon, Hong Kong [5/2021]

Contents

Essential Element: Physical Systems

Essential Element: Human Systems

Contents, continued

A Globe

Concept:
A globe is a geographic representation of Earth.

Mrs. Takagawa asks Emily to come up to the front of her class. "Spin the globe," she says with a broad smile. Emily swipes two fingers across it and the small circular model of the world spins around. Mrs. Takagawa says, "Now place your finger on a spot and make it stop." Emily presses her finger down and skids the globe to a stop on a landmark on Earth. "Can you name that spot?" her teacher asks. Emily inspects the exact location where her finger is and reads, "The Indian Ocean." Mrs. Takagawa looks at the globe and replies, "Very good, Emily! The Indian Ocean is one of the five oceans on our planet."

Next, Emily's classmate Ben gives it a try. His finger lands on the Arctic. Maggie goes next. Her finger stops on North America—the Rocky Mountains to be exact. The next person spins and lands on the continent of Asia. Each time a person takes a turn, he or she says the location on the globe and Mrs. Takagawa shares a fact about that place. At the end of the lesson, Mrs. Takagawa says, "Now let's learn about Earth and specific locations or regions shown on the globe. Get ready for a wonderful journey. We will discover many great places on our planet!"

The World in Spatial Terms

About Globes

Concept:
A globe is a geographic representation of Earth.

The World in Spatial Terms

A globe is a small circular, or spherical, model of Earth. The Earth is shaped like a ball and so is the globe, except a globe is hollow. The globe shows the largest landmasses on Earth called continents. Most globes also show many of the nearly 200 countries on Earth. A globe shows where the oceans are, Earth's five largest bodies of water. Globes have an imaginary line called the equator that splits the Earth in half. On some globes there are lines that run east to west above and below the equator. These are called parallels or lines of latitude. There are also lines that run up and down or north to south. These are called lines of longitude or meridians. Both sets of lines help people find exact locations on Earth.

Some globes also show large mountain ranges, inland seas, long rivers, and very large lakes. A few major cities are usually shown on globes as well. When people need to see more detailed information about locations on Earth, they use a map.

Define It!

globe: a small circular and hollow scale model of the Earth that spins around

continent: one of seven large areas of land on Earth

equator: the imaginary line on Earth that splits it in half

Answer the items.

1. When you look at a globe, do you see more water or land?

_____

2. Where do you live on Earth? _____
   Find your exact location and describe it to someone.

3. Would you rather own a map or a globe? Explain your answer.

_____

_____

ALL About Globes

lines of latitude

equator

lines of Longitude

The World in Spatial Terms

Concept:
A globe is a geographic representation of Earth.

Earth from Space

Define It!

atmosphere: the air and other gases that surround Earth

storm: a weather event caused by low pressure that brings clouds and rain and strong winds

poles: the two areas at the very top and bottom of Earth

Earth is visible from space. Space is anywhere beyond Earth's atmosphere. Our atmosphere is made up of the air and other gases that surround Earth. When looking at our planet from space, several things become clear. First, the Earth is mostly water. About 71% of the Earth's surface is water. Second, there is also water in the Earth's atmosphere. You can see this water in the swirling white areas of clouds above the planet. Clouds are actually billions of water droplets suspended, or hanging, in the air. An occurrence of bad weather in which there is a lot of rain, snow, or strong winds is a storm. Storms are always in motion because the Earth is constantly spinning. If you take a picture of the Earth today, it will look different tomorrow. The clouds and storms will change in shape and size and be in a new location.

It is clear from space that the Earth is round. It has two poles—the one at its northernmost point is called the North Pole. The one at its southernmost point is called the South Pole.

Answer the items.

1. Describe Earth's atmosphere.

   _____

2. If you took a picture of Earth from space on two different days, how might the pictures look different?

   _____

   _____

Skill Sharpeners: Geography • EMC 3743 • © Evan-Moor Corp.

The World in Spatial Terms

Our Planet

©NASA

This is a picture of planet Earth and its moon taken from space.

Skill:
Apply content vocabulary in context sentences

All About Earth

Read each clue and write the missing word on the line.

Earth	storms	atmosphere	equator
poles	continent	water	globe

1. A large area of land on Earth is called a _____.

2. The air that surrounds Earth is its _____.

3. A circular scale model of the Earth that spins is a _____.

4. The very top and bottom of Earth are its two _____.

5. The imaginary line that divides Earth in half

   is called the _____.

6. Weather events that cause wind, clouds, and rain

   are called _____.

7. The planet on which we live is called _____.

8. Most of Earth is covered with _____.

Think About It

Do you think more people live above or below the equator? Why?

_____

_____

_____

Skill Sharpeners: Geography • EMC 3743 • © Evan-Moor Corp.

The World in Spatial Terms

Model of a Planet

Use paper to create a model of a planet that is similar to Earth.

Skill:
Apply geography concepts in context

The World in Spatial Terms

What You Need

- one large sheet of light blue construction paper
- light brown construction paper
- white construction paper
- ruler and pencil
- scissors
- string or yarn
- glue and tape

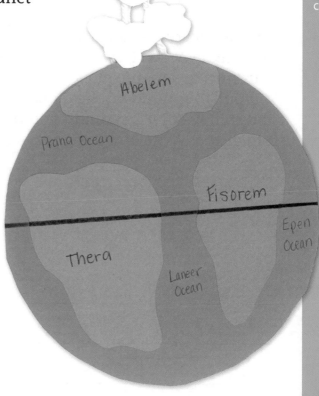

What You Do

1. Place the light blue paper on a flat surface. Using a large flat, circular object, trace one circle. This will be your planet.

2. Use the light brown paper to cut out three to five various-sized continents for your planet. Remember, continents are large areas of land. But also remember, like Earth, your planet needs to be mostly water. Glue the continents to both sides of your planet.

3. Using the ruler, add an equator to both sides of your planet.

4. Using the pencil, write the names of your continents and oceans.

5. Tape a string to your planet. Add storms by cutting and gluing small pieces of white paper to the string. Remember, these areas of clouds are small in comparison to the whole planet.

6. Name your planet and show it to your family.

My Finger Landed...

Pretend you are a student in Mrs. Takagawa's class. It is your turn to spin the globe. You put your hand on the globe and spin it. After 2 seconds, you put your finger on it and it skids it to a stop. Write about the location your finger lands on.

- Where is it on Earth?
- Is it on land or in the ocean?
- Is it near the equator?

_____

_____

_____

_____

_____

_____

_____

_____

_____

_____

Skill:
Write explanatory text to convey information clearly

The World in Spatial Terms

Skill Sharpeners: Geography • EMC 3743 • © Evan-Moor Corp.

Concept:
Cardinal and intermediate directions are used to describe places and locations.

Chasing a Tornado

The driver turns around and grins at you and your family. "We are about to witness the spectacular!" she says. The storm comes quickly. "The tornado is touching the ground to our east," the driver shouts. Everyone in the car looks in that direction. The massive, swirling cloud is spinning a funnel all the way to the ground. The driver then says, "It's now moving to the northeast." Everyone watches in awe as the swirling tornado kicks up a giant dust cloud on the ground.

The other storm chaser in front looks at his map. "Just up ahead, Laramie Road should get us behind the storm from the southwest," he says. "Turn there!" From the back seat you ask, "What if the tornado comes toward us?" The driver replies, "We're experts at this. We know where tornadoes typically move in the United States—from the southwest to the northeast. We are watching this one very closely. We promise we'll keep you safe!"

The tornado heads just where the experts said it would. Your mom says, "I am so glad you knew where it would go."

"They don't always cooperate," the driver says. "But this one did!" Everyone watches as the tornado spins northeast toward a cornfield, tearing up crops along the way.

The World in Spatial Terms

Finding Directions

The World in Spatial Terms

Define It!

cardinal directions: the directions of north, south, east, and west

intermediate directions: the four in-between directions, northwest (NW), northeast (NE), southeast (SE), and southwest (SW)

Maps show two kinds of directions. Cardinal directions are the four main directions. They are north, south, east, and west. North points up on a map, and south points down. West is to the left and east is to the right. A compass rose shows these directions on the map.

Intermediate directions are in-between the cardinal directions. These are northwest (NW), northeast (NE), southwest (SW), and southeast (SE). All of these directions help people in emergencies, such as avoiding a tornado. Directions are also needed to find a route to and from school or a store. They may help locate a lost dog, fight a fire, plan a long hike, and many other things. Knowing how to read and understand directions is very important!

Answer the items.

1. Who might use cardinal directions to do a job? Explain your answer.

   _____

   _____

2. Which kind of direction do you think is more helpful: cardinal or intermediate? Explain your answer.

   _____

   _____

   _____

Skill Sharpeners: Geography • EMC 3743 • © Evan-Moor Corp.

A compass rose

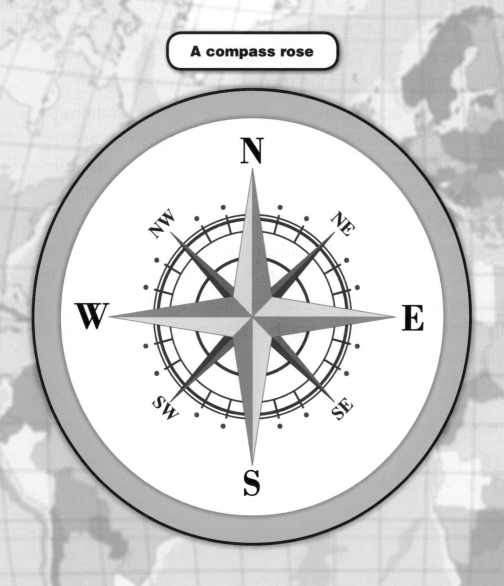

Tornado Movement

Concept:
Cardinal and intermediate directions are used to describe places and locations.

The World in Spatial Terms

Define It!

tornado: a rapidly spinning column of air that reaches from a stormcloud all the way to the ground

storm chaser: a person trained to safely follow storms to photograph and study them

Tornadoes occur nearly everywhere on Earth. The area where they happen the most is in the middle of the United States. This area is called Tornado Alley because of the many large tornadoes there.

In Tornado Alley, storms usually move from the southwest (SW) to the northeast (NE). Every tornado is different, and its movement cannot always be predicted. Some things that can make a storm move differently are areas of water, mountain ranges, and erratic, or changing, wind patterns.

Storm chasers know typical tornado movements, and they watch each storm carefully. Chasers use maps and know to follow tornadoes from behind at a safe distance. This means that storm chasers locate themselves southwest or behind the tornado as it moves toward the northeast.

Answer the items.

1. Describe how you or someone you know used directions to go somewhere.

   _____

   _____

2. If you had to predict the path of a tornado, what information could you use to help make your prediction?

   _____

   _____

Skill Sharpeners: Geography • EMC 3743 • © Evan-Moor Corp.

A team of storm chasers is watching a tornado.

A tornado chaser is tracking a storm on the radar screen.

A truck is equipped with special tools to measure the strength of the storm.

The World in Spatial Terms

Tornado Words

Find these tornado words in the word search.
Hint: Some are backwards.

cardinal	directions	intermediate	tornado
tornado alley	storm chaser	compass rose	

c	c	r	l	t	y	d	l	r	m	s	t	s	c	z
a	i	t	e	d	y	a	g	x	m	o	l	n	d	j
x	g	m	u	s	n	i	q	i	r	b	i	o	g	u
b	n	j	r	i	a	p	k	n	j	s	j	i	y	k
n	f	x	d	a	q	h	a	b	c	t	r	t	n	l
y	m	r	y	t	s	d	c	o	i	s	s	c	c	v
c	a	i	y	h	o	e	b	m	s	o	o	e	f	n
c	i	s	l	a	f	p	g	d	r	f	p	r	p	h
k	e	o	l	t	o	r	n	a	d	o	m	i	z	k
i	c	l	k	l	q	d	q	w	c	v	t	d	t	c
u	e	v	c	o	m	p	a	s	s	r	o	s	e	m
y	n	i	t	v	r	l	t	c	m	k	z	c	n	e
e	t	a	i	d	e	m	r	e	t	n	i	h	s	k
u	y	j	r	i	j	d	i	u	d	u	e	l	a	b
v	f	p	o	s	r	z	k	l	v	p	n	j	n	o

Skill Sharpeners: Geography • EMC 3743 • © Evan-Moor Corp.

Skill: Use visual discrimination

The World in Spatial Terms

Mapping a Tornado

Trace a map that shows the path and direction of a tornado.

Skill:
Apply geography skills in real-world tasks

What You Need

- computer with Internet access
- map of location where there was a tornado
- ruler
- red pencil or highlighter
- sheet of paper

path of tornado

What You Do

1. Find a location where a tornado has touched down. You can find this information on an international or national weather website. Print out a map of the city or town.

2. Find out where the tornado first touched the ground, how long it was on the ground, and the path it took.

3. Use a ruler and pencil or highlighter to trace the tornado's path on the map. Mark where it first touched down with an **X**.

4. On a sheet of paper, write in which direction the twister traveled. Write whether it was in a cardinal or an intermediate direction or both. Write how long it was on the ground. Then show someone the tornado's path on the map and tell him or her information about it.

The World in Spatial Terms

The World in Spatial Terms

You Are in Charge!

Pretend you are traveling with a group of storm chasers and you are the expert. Your job is to make sure everyone is safe.

- What should you do?
- What would you say to make everyone feel safe?
- What can you tell the others about tornadoes?

_____

_____

_____

_____

_____

_____

_____

_____

_____

_____

Practice Drill

Concept:
Maps are created to communicate specific information.

The Mathews family is gathered in the living room. "OK," Mr. Mathews announces, "we are going to pretend there is an emergency and evacuate the house. We reviewed our evacuation map last night. After I sound the alarm, do what we rehearsed." The thought of a real emergency was scary to Kyle and Lauren Mathews, the youngest kids in the Mathews family. Lauren whispers to Kyle as they go upstairs to their bedrooms, "I'm glad this is only a practice drill."

As planned, each member of the family lies on their beds wearing their pajamas. Soon the whistle blows. They jump up and grab their emergency bags, which contain a jacket and an extra set of clothes. Lauren finds their cat Mittens hiding under the bed and grabs her as she shuffles quickly into the hall. The rest of the family is running quickly, getting everything they need. Kyle dashes downstairs and notices the fishbowl is gone. He realizes that everyone is doing their jobs.

Finally, the Mathews family members go outside to the front yard, their agreed upon meeting place. Mr. Mathews announces, "Not bad, 38 seconds. But in the event of a fire, we may have to get out much faster. We will practice again tomorrow!"

The World in Spatial Terms

The World in Spatial Terms

Tornado Alley

People who live in South Dakota, Nebraska, Kansas, Oklahoma, and Texas experience a lot of big storms. Many people call these areas of the United States Tornado Alley. People who live in Tornado Alley have to be prepared for big storms. Many towns in Tornado Alley have warning sirens located throughout the city. When a tornado is approaching, the sirens are sounded so the people can immediately go to a safer area. Most people who live in Tornado Alley have basements or storm shelters to take shelter in during a storm. These rooms are below the ground and are much less likely to get damaged during a tornado. If a house does not have a basement, people may find shelter in a hallway in the middle of the house away from windows. In some cases, when the tornado sirens are sounded early enough, people leave town. Many families prepare for this by drawing evacuation routes so they will know which roads or highways will get them away from the storm quickly.

Schools in Tornado Alley also prepare for tornadoes. One very important safety procedure at a school is to get to the safest building on campus. That building is usually located in the middle of the school. After students are there, they crouch down and use their hands to protect their heads and necks. More injuries come from flying objects during a tornado than anything else.

Answer the item.

What are the most important things to do during a tornado?

_____

_____

_____

Skill Sharpeners: Geography • EMC 3743 • © Evan-Moor Corp.

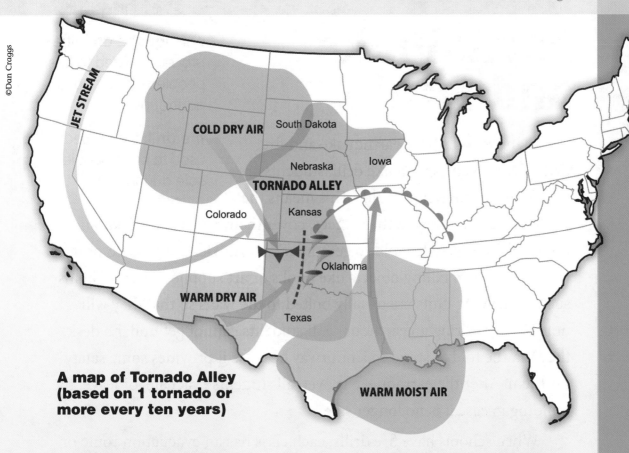

©Dan Craggs

JET STREAM

COLD DRY AIR   South Dakota

Nebraska   Iowa

TORNADO ALLEY

Colorado   Kansas

Oklahoma

WARM DRY AIR

Texas

WARM MOIST AIR

**A map of Tornado Alley
(based on 1 tornado or
more every ten years)**

**A tornado
warning siren**

STORM
ZONE

**A storm zone sign
on the roadside**

**A tornado approaching
a house**

The World in Spatial Terms

The World in Spatial Terms

Earthquake and Fire!

Define It!

earthquake drill: the procedure used to keep people safe during an earthquake

fire drill: the procedure used to keep people safe during a fire

Many schools have earthquake and fire drills. During an earthquake drill, students are told to "drop, cover, and hold." This means that students need to drop to their knees, cover their heads and necks, and hold still. They are also told to get under a sturdy desk or table to protect themselves from falling objects like books or art supplies. Heavier items such as shelving units are usually bolted to the walls so that they will not fall over during an earthquake. If students cannot get under a desk, they may be told to stand in a doorway because it provides some safety for them. After the earthquake is over, all students evacuate, or leave, the building in case it is no longer safe.

When schools have fire drills, each class has an evacuation route or a plan to follow. The students and teachers and anyone else who works at the school practice what to do if there is a fire. The drill begins when the fire alarm rings. Students line up and quietly follow their teacher to the safe place that is shown on the fire escape route map. Schools' leaders make the fire escape route maps by planning the best way for everyone at the school to get out of the buildings safely. The routes are reviewed by school leaders and sometimes even the fire department to make sure they are the best ones possible for a real emergency.

Answer the item.

What might the fire department look for during a fire drill to make sure it was safe?

_____

_____

_____

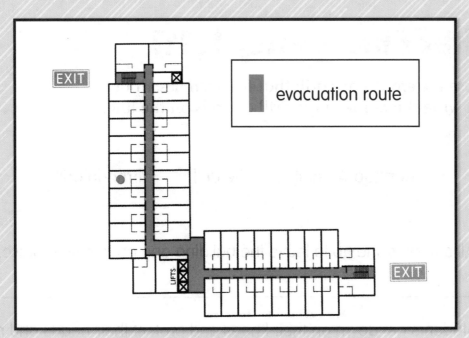

An evacuation route in a school building

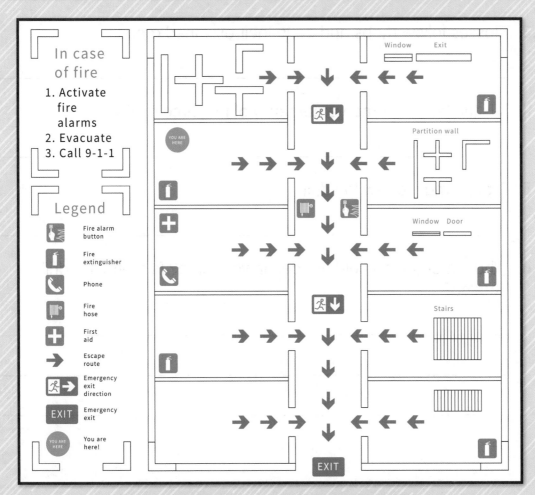

An evacuation route for a large building

The World in Spatial Terms

Skill:
Apply content vocabulary in context sentences

What Emergency Is It?

Choose the emergency drill that fits each description.
Then write the name of the drill or drills on the line.

earthquake drill	fire drill	tornado drill

1. All students line up to leave the building and go to a safe place.

   _____

2. Students get down on their knees and protect their heads and necks.

   _____

3. Classes follow maps and go to their assigned areas.

   _____

4. It is the least common emergency of the three choices.

   _____

5. Experts may review the drill.

   _____

6. What emergency could happen in your area? Is a practice drill needed?

   _____

   _____

   _____

The World in Spatial Terms

Home Evacuation

Make a map of your house and draw an emergency evacuation route.

Skill:
Apply concepts in real-world tasks

What You Need

- red pencil
- paper
- ruler
- stopwatch

What You Do

1. Draw a bird's-eye map of your house. That means that you draw it as if you are looking down at your house but it does not have a roof. If there are two levels to your house, make two separate drawings. One of the bottom floor and one of the top floor.

2. Draw details in each room such as windows, doors, and furniture.

3. Next, draw evacuation plans on the map to show where each family member would go in an emergency. Trace a line with arrows from where each person starts the evacuation to where they end up.

4. After you finish the map, share it with your family. Then practice the evacuation with your family, having someone time the drill from when it starts to when everyone meets outside.

5. Practice the drill at least once a year so your family will be well-prepared in case of an emergency.

The World in Spatial Terms

Skill:
Write and reflect
for the purpose
of planning

Be Prepared!

Think about the things you and your family
may need to be prepared for an emergency.
Make a shopping list of things for your family
to buy so you can create an emergency kit.

Shopping List
for Our Emergency Kit

_____

_____

_____

_____

_____

_____

_____

_____

_____

_____

_____

Getting to School

Concept:
Data from different sources are used to create maps.

"If we walk to school, we could walk along First Avenue. That is the shortest route," Krista points out to her mom on the map.

"But it is almost two miles and I'll be carrying my supplies," says her mom, who teaches at the school.

"What if we ride our bikes?" Krista asks. "That could save time, and I could loan you a backpack to hold your supplies."

Krista's mom looks at the map again. "Not on First Avenue. It is too busy in the morning. We could ride over here though." Her mom points out a small pathway winding through the park. "That's the bike path, and it is car free."

"But it is farther away," Krista protests. "The time we'd save riding our bikes instead of walking will be lost."

"You could always drive the car!" Krista's dad chimes in with a smirk.

"Not on Earth Day!" Krista and her mom and her brother Harry chant in unison.

"Let's just leave a little earlier and ride our bikes through the park," Mom concludes. "Although the bike path is a longer route, it is the safest route to ride to school. Harry and Dad, you can help us celebrate Earth Day by riding your bikes, too!"

The World in Spatial Terms

Concept:
Data from different sources are used to create maps.

Transportation Options

Define It!

transportation: getting from one place to another

carbon footprint: things you do that pollute or hurt the Earth and its atmosphere

light rail: shorter train routes in towns and cities

There are many ways to get from one place to another in cities and towns.

You can walk, but walking can take a long time if you are going somewhere far away. Biking is another choice. It is good exercise and saves gas. Many people choose to ride a bike because they want to reduce their carbon footprint. That means they don't want to pollute the air by using a gas-powered car. But some routes may not be safe to ride a bike. Because of this, many towns have created bike paths.

Driving by car is another option, especially if you need to get somewhere fast. But some families do not have cars. In that case, a bus may be the best way to get from one place to another. But if there are a lot of stops on the route, a bus may not be the fastest way. In larger cities and towns, light rail is a good way to get from place to place. Light rail is a train that travels short distances very quickly. The train travels on its own special tracks, so there is no traffic to get in its way.

Answer the items.

1. Which transportation options reduce your carbon footprint?

   _____

2. Which transportation option is best for getting somewhere fast?

   _____

3. Do you like to walk, bike, or ride in a vehicle to get to school? Explain your answer.

   _____

Skill Sharpeners: Geography • EMC 3743 • © Evan-Moor Corp.

This map shows walking and driving transportation options.

This infographic shows a variety of transportation options.

The World in Spatial Terms

Transportation Maps

Concept:
Data from different sources are used to create maps.

The World in Spatial Terms

Define It!

destination: a place a person is traveling to

ground transportation: cars, buses, and trains used to travel from one location to another

symbol: a picture that stands for something

People who are traveling long distances have many options. Some people choose to drive a vehicle. They must think about the route they will take and how much time it will take to get to their final destination. People who are traveling long distances may choose to fly. Most countries have international airports in large cities. People who travel by air fly with hundreds of other passengers and may have to take more than one flight to get to their final destination. Some people prefer to travel by train. Train stations are usually located in large cities. Traveling by boat is another option. Boats take passengers across bays and oceans, and through canals, or man-made waterways.

Sometimes, people have to take more than one type of transportation to get to their final destination. For example, a person who wants to go to Monterey, California, might fly to San Francisco airport and then take ground transportation, such as a shuttle or a rental car, and drive two hours south to Monterey. Many cities have bus and subway systems or light rails that take people to locations in the city or nearby cities. Transportation options are shown on maps with symbols that show the travel choices available in each area.

Answer the items.

1. When is ground transportation used?

   _____

2. What is the best way to travel long distances?

   _____

Transportation Map

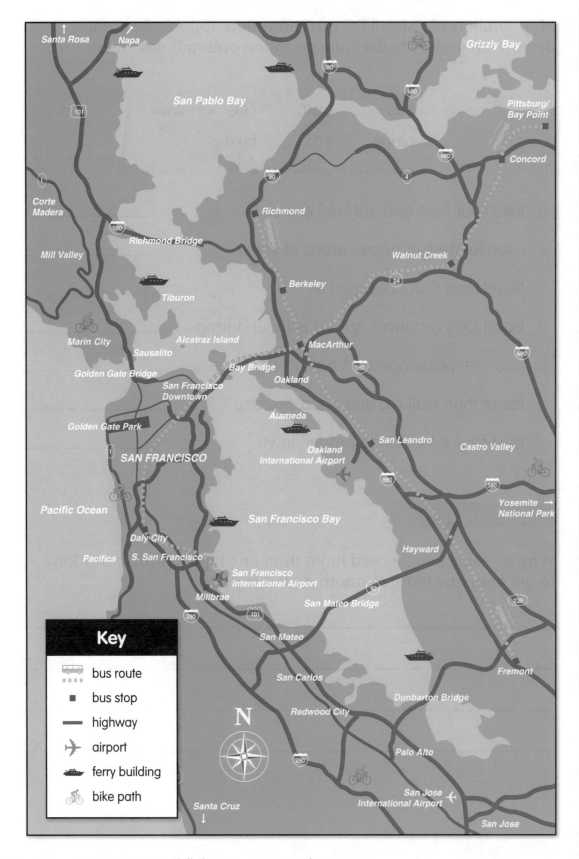

The World in Spatial Terms

Skill:
Apply geography concepts

Types of Transportation

Map symbols can stand for transportation options. Read the description and write the transportation option it describes.

bus	boat	car	walk
plane	train	bike	

1. take your time and get light exercise _____

2. used for getting across areas of water _____

3. travel long distances quickly _____

4. travel long distances quickly without driving _____

5. ride with passengers on a short city route _____

6. faster than walking and good exercise _____

7. best choice for driving around town _____

Think About It

Why do some people need more than one type of transportation to get from one place to another on a trip?

_____

_____

_____

_____

The World in Spatial Terms

Skill Sharpeners: Geography • EMC 3743 • © Evan-Moor Corp.

A Town's Transportation Map

Skill:
Apply geography concepts in real-world tasks

Make a map of a town. Use symbols to show different transportation options.

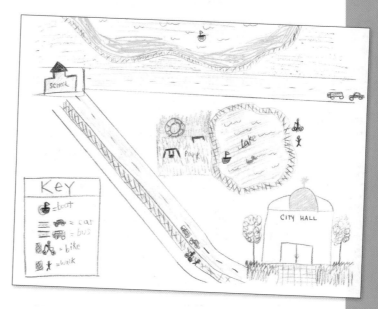

What You Need

- large sheet of light colored construction paper
- ruler
- colored pencils

What You Do

1. Draw a map of an area in your town or in another town on the construction paper. Include major streets, parks, schools, water areas such as lakes and rivers, and landmarks such as City Hall. Think about the transportation options that are available to get from place to place.

2. Draw a map key in the bottom left corner of your map. Make symbols for the transportation options in your town. Some examples are bike, walk, bus, car, train, and boat.

3. Then draw transportation routes on your map that show how to get from one place to another. Draw the transportation symbol beside each route.

The World in Spatial Terms

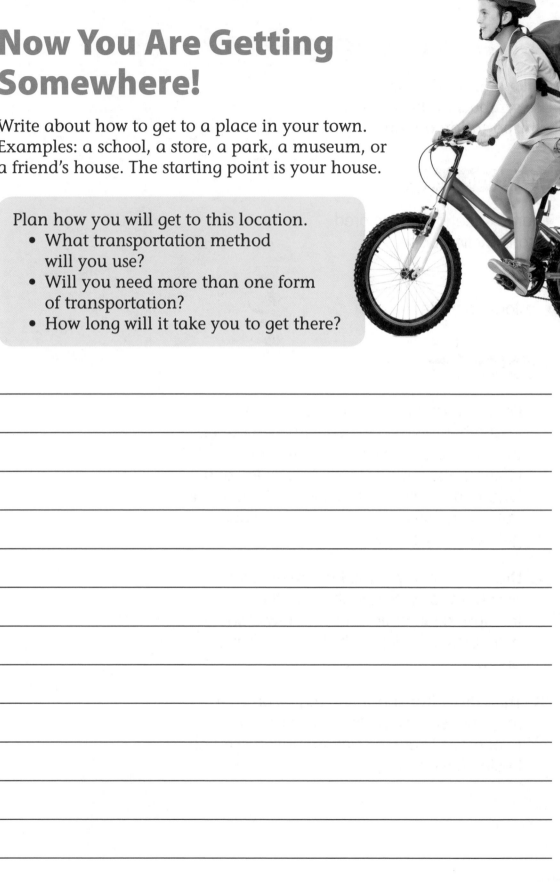

Now You Are Getting Somewhere!

Write about how to get to a place in your town. Examples: a school, a store, a park, a museum, or a friend's house. The starting point is your house.

Plan how you will get to this location.
- What transportation method will you use?
- Will you need more than one form of transportation?
- How long will it take you to get there?

_____

_____

_____

_____

_____

_____

_____

_____

_____

_____

_____

Concept:
Places are locations that have distinct physical and human characteristics.

The Top of the World!

My dad has a lot of stories about his travels. This is one of them.

"We were well above 20,000 feet elevation. The sun was glaring down on us, reflecting off the snow. I could hardly breathe, but at least we had oxygen canisters with us. I was very thankful for the guides on our journey. They helped carry all of our equipment. They are much better at that elevation than I am.

There were times I wanted to give up. My steps were incredibly slow and difficult. But then the clouds cleared and there I was staring at Everest, the tallest mountain in the world. The top of the mountain was all rock and snow and really steep. I could see a plume of snow blowing off the peak. I still had a ways to go—but after seeing it, I knew I just had to reach the top."

Dad stopped for a moment to think about climbing the highest mountain on Earth. Then he told us about what it was like on the summit.

"From up there," Dad said, *"I was looking down on everything. Below me was a sea of clouds, other snowcapped peaks, and valleys far, far down. I was on top of the world."*

Places and Regions

Mountains All Over Earth

Concept:
Places are locations that have distinct physical and human characteristics.

Define It!

mountain range: a group of connected mountains

glacier: a large body of ice that moves slowly

Mt. Everest is the tallest mountain in the world. It is 29,029 feet (8,848 m) high. Mt. Everest is part of the Himalaya Mountains of Asia. This mountain range has the ten highest peaks in the world, including Everest. The Himalayas are in the countries of India, Nepal, Bhutan, Tibet, Pakistan, and Afghanistan. This region is known for frigid weather at high elevations and massive glaciers.

There are other major mountain ranges on Earth. The rugged Alps of Europe stretch into eight countries, including Switzerland, Austria, Germany, and France. The Andes of South America are the longest mountain range in the world. They are in seven countries, including Chile, Ecuador, Argentina, and Peru. The Rocky Mountains of North America stretch from the southwest of the United States to northern British Columbia in Canada. Another very well-known mountain range is the Sierra Nevada in eastern California. Sierra Nevada is Spanish for "snowy range." Just north of the Sierras is the Cascade Range of volcanoes that stretch from northern California to southern British Columbia, Canada.

Answer the items.

1. What do the mountain ranges in the text have in common?

_____

_____

2. Would you like to visit the longest mountain range in the world or the highest? Explain your answer.

_____

_____

Places and Regions

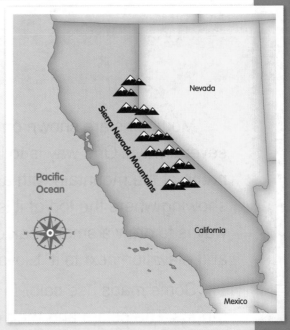

The Sierra Nevada mountain range

The Andes mountain range

Mt. Everest in the Himalaya mountain range

The Alps mountain range

Places and Regions

Mountains on a Map

Define It!

peak: the very top of a mountain

elevation: the height above sea level

contour lines: lines that show the steepness of a mountain

Mountains are shown on maps in several ways. One way is to have the name of the mountain with a **+** mark showing where the top of it is. Another way is to draw a small peak on the map and write its name and elevation next to it. Elevation is how tall the mountain is.

Some maps use color to show mountains or mountain ranges. The colors and their elevations are explained in a map key. Sometimes, mountains are just shaded to show where they are. Also, some maps may show a coating of white on the peaks of the mountains to show snow or glaciers on them.

Some maps use contour lines to show mountains and mountain ranges. The lines are either close together or far apart to show how steep or gradual the elevation gain is on the mountain. Maps with lines like this are called topographical maps.

Answer the items.

1. What kind of information can you get about a mountain from a map?

   _____

   _____

2. What do the lines on the topographical map above show you?

   _____

Places and Regions

40

North America

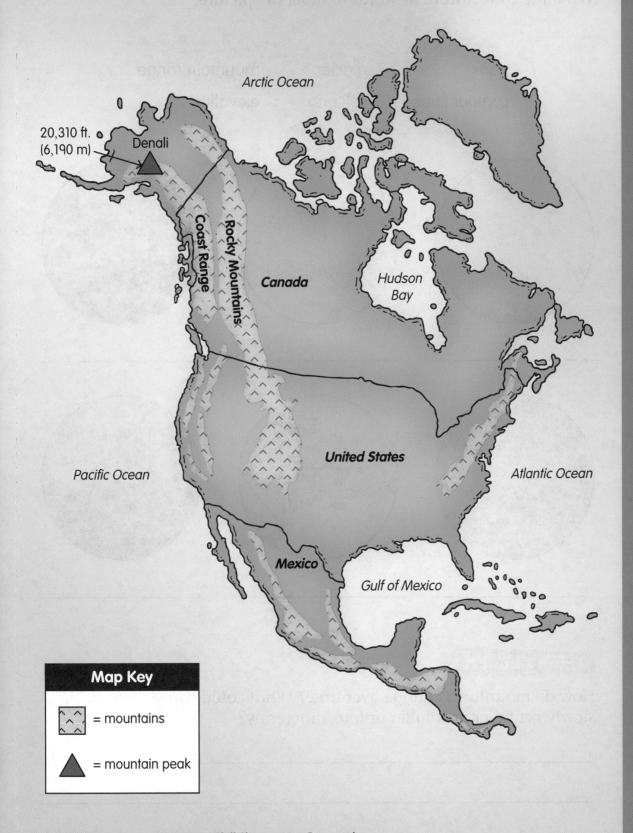

Arctic Ocean

20,310 ft.
(6,190 m) Denali

Coast Range

Rocky Mountains

Canada

Hudson Bay

Pacific Ocean

United States

Atlantic Ocean

Mexico

Gulf of Mexico

Map Key

= mountains

= mountain peak

Places and Regions

Mountain Parts

Write the correct word or words to label the picture.

peak	glacier	mountain range
contour lines	volcano	elevation

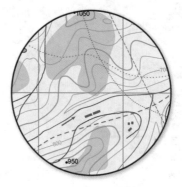

_____

_____

_____

5,862 feet

_____

_____

_____

Think About It

How do mountains change over time? What could cause them to slowly get taller or smaller or look differently?

_____

_____

Skill Sharpeners: Geography • EMC 3743 • © Evan-Moor Corp.

Rocky Mountains

Draw a landscape of the Rocky Mountains.

Skill:
Create representations of geographic features

What You Need

• large sheet of white paper

• colored pencils

Rocky Mountains

What You Do

1. Look at the photo of the Rocky Mountains. Trace the lines of the mountains with your finger.

2. Decide which part of the picture you will draw first. Use your pencils to sketch the outlines of both the mountains and the valley below. Then finish your drawing by coloring the picture.

Places and Regions

Skill:
Write informative text to convey information and experiences clearly

To the Top of the Mountain!

About 800 people try to climb to the top of Mt. Everest each year. Pretend that you are one of the few who reach the summit. Write a journal entry that tells about the climb, how you felt when you reached the top, and what you saw.

Places and Regions

44

On the Water

Concept:
Places are locations that have distinct physical and human characteristics.

I have been interested in rivers since I was a young kid. I grew up near a creek and I would visit it often. I would watch the water rise and rush along in winter, and then slow to a trickle in summer.

As an adult, I went on a journey canoeing one of the world's most famous rivers, the Mississippi. The Mississippi is the fourth-longest river in the world, traveling 2,340 miles (3,766 km). People have explored it for centuries. The Mississippi begins in northern Minnesota as a small body of water. It slowly meanders along, growing larger as it flows toward the Gulf of Mexico.

A barge on the Mississippi River in Baton Rouge, Louisiana

I shared my journey with many man-made parts of the river. There were cities and factories all along the way. Sometimes, people were fishing from small boats or canoes. Many huge boats called barges carrying goods would pass by. I had to stay far away from them to make sure I was safe.

The river was next to a lot of farms. I could see the sprinklers running, watering the crops. I wondered how much water was taken out of the Mississippi. Even though I was always surrounded by water, I had to stop and buy drinking water in the towns along the banks. The water in the river was too polluted to drink

I still remember the first day of my journey. I was at the very start, or the headwaters, of the Mississippi. My friends pushed my canoe into the water. I waved goodbye, venturing out on my own. I was set to canoe the river all the way until it reached its end at the Gulf of Mexico. There the Mississippi forms into a delta, or an area of spread-out flat water and land, much different than at the start. My journey would take me two months to complete.

The Mighty Mississippi

Concept:
Places are locations that have distinct physical and human characteristics.

A great deal of the land around the Mississippi today is farmland. Farms take water from the river to water their crops. This is called irrigation. Many of those farms use fertilizer and other chemical products to help grow their crops. Some of the waste from that has gone into the Mississippi. Because of this, the water is no longer as clear and clean as it used to be.

The river is used by a lot of boats. Many of them are large boats called barges.

The water of the Mississippi no longer flows freely. All along the river are a series of dams. These were built to generate electricity. Dams also help set up areas on the water for outdoor activities such as boating and fishing. Even though the Mississippi is no longer a freely running wild river, it is still huge! Several large rivers, including the Missouri, Ohio, and Arkansas, feed into it. By the time the Mississippi reaches the Gulf of Mexico, it is the fourth-largest river (measured by the amount of water it pours into the ocean) in the world.

Define It!

irrigation: moving water from one place to another

fertilizer: chemical and natural products given to crops to help their growth

barge: a long boat with a flat bottom used for carrying goods

dam: a man-made structure that blocks river water from flowing

tributaries: rivers that flow into another river, making it grow larger

Answer the items.

1. Do you think farmers should be allowed to grow crops along the Mississippi? Explain your answer.

_____

2. What can you learn about the Mississippi River by looking at the photos and the map?

_____

Places and Regions

Skill Sharpeners: Geography • EMC 3743 • © Evan-Moor Corp.

These barges are in the Chain of Rocks Canal on the Mississippi River.

This photo shows where the Missouri and Mississippi Rivers meet.

Places and Regions

The Blue Danube

Concept:
Places are locations that have distinct physical and human characteristics.

Define It!

fortress: a fort used by the military to secure an area

hydroelectric: using moving water to make electricity

tourist: a person who is on vacation in a certain area

The Danube River in Europe has an even longer history than the Mississippi. Along its route are remains of some of the earliest human settlements. Near it are castles and fortresses built hundreds of years ago. The river was once an important border for countries of the past.

The Danube is the second-longest river in Europe. It travels 1,777 miles (2,860 km) from Germany to the Black Sea. It passes through parts of ten countries, including Germany, Austria, Hungary, and Romania.

Just like the Mississippi, the Danube supplies water for people and farms. There are also hydroelectric dams on the Danube that generate electricity. Another use of the river is to transport goods on boats.

Finally, the Danube is known as a scenic river. Several of the beautiful cities it passes include Ulm in Germany, Vienna in Austria, and Budapest in Hungary. These cities are known as popular tourist areas where people take vacations. Many people take cruises on the Danube, and there are many miles of bike paths along its shores.

Answer the items.

1. If you went on a Danube River cruise, what would you want to see the most?

   _____

2. In what ways are the Danube and the Mississippi similar?

Places and Regions

48

**View of Ulm along the
Danube River in Germany**

**The Danube River and the
Vienna skyline in Austria**

**View of the Budapest Parliament in
Hungary, overlooking the Danube River**

Germany

Danube River

Ulm ★

Vienna ★

Austria

Budapest ★

Slovakia

Hungary

Croatia

Serbia

Romania

Bulgaria

Places and Regions

Skill:
Apply content
vocabulary in
context

River Words

Use these words to label the pictures.

barge	dam	canoe
castle	irrigation	farm

_____ _____ _____

_____ _____ _____

Think About It

What interests you the most about life along the banks of a river?

_____

_____

Skill Sharpeners: Geography • EMC 3743 • © Evan-Moor Corp.

A River Scene

In this activity, you will create a river scene that shows the activities that take place on a river and the buildings and communities found along it.

What You Need

- drawings, sketches, or photos of small boats, barges, dams, bikes, farms, castles, etc.

- scratch paper

- poster board

- glue

- pencil and colored pencils or markers

What You Do

1. On a sheet of scratch paper, sketch a river scene. Plan where you will put features such as buildings, river activities, and dams.

2. When you have finished your sketch, copy it onto the poster board.

3. Gather the materials you will need for your scene. Will you draw the pictures? Will you print photos from the Internet? Make sure that your drawings or the photos you choose will fit in your river scene.

4. Glue all your drawings and/or photos in place. Consider adding other features such as more boats, people fishing, animals in the water, or castles and fortresses. Make your river a busy place.

5. Name your river and show your scene to your family!

Places and Regions

Water Near You

What body of water is near your town? Does your community use it for recreation, as a water source, or both? Think about what you know. Then ask your parents to help you find more information about a major river or lake near your town. Write about it and how it is used.

_____

_____

_____

_____

_____

_____

_____

_____

_____

_____

_____

Places and Regions

Concept:
Physical processes shape features on Earth's surface.

Super Volcano

My family and I visited Yellowstone National Park some years ago. We were fascinated by the fact that Yellowstone was the first national park in the world. Upon arriving, we quickly set up our tent at the campground, and then rushed off to a "ranger talk" to learn more about the park. The ranger started speaking about what happened at Yellowstone long before it was ever a national park.

"About 600,000 years ago, a huge volcanic eruption occurred right here at Yellowstone. Because of that super volcano, most of the Earth's crust was blown away here. That left the Yellowstone area with some of the thinnest crust on the planet. That means the hot core, or center of the Earth, isn't that far below where we are now.

Water trickles below the Earth's surface from rain or snow. It reaches that hot core, heats up, and rises back up to the surface as hot-water spots called thermals. There are over 10,000 of them here at Yellowstone—making this place the coolest hot place on Earth."

My family and I looked at each other with big eyes—this was going to be some camping trip!

Physical Systems

Yellowstone Is Hot!

Concept:
Physical processes shape features on Earth's surface.

Define It!

caldera: a collapsed volcano

fumarole: a hole in the ground that lets out steam and other gases

geyser: a place where very hot to boiling water sprays out of the ground

The ground beneath Yellowstone National Park is part of a caldera, or a collapsed volcano. The eruption that occurred at Yellowstone just over 600,000 years ago made the crust, or top layer of the Earth, there incredibly thin.

Hot water beneath the ground at Yellowstone rises up toward the Earth's surface. It reaches the surface in amazing ways. The most famous hot-water feature at the park is Old Faithful Geyser. A geyser is where boiling water sprays up out of the ground. Old Faithful Geyser shoots water up to 180 feet (55 m) into the air once every hour or so. There are over 300 geysers at Yellowstone. There are also many steam vents called fumaroles. These are places where steam hisses through a hole in the ground. Yellowstone also has deep, hot pools and large boiling springs. There are also pits of boiling and plopping mud.

There are over 10,000 of these hot-water features at Yellowstone, which is more than any place in the world. Many people come from all over the world to see them.

Answer the items.

1. Why is there so much hot water coming out of the ground at Yellowstone?

_____

_____

2. How would you make sure visitors stay safe around the hot water?

_____

_____

Physical Systems

Skill Sharpeners: Geography • EMC 3743 • © Evan-Moor Corp.

Old Faithful during summer in Yellowstone National Park, Wyoming

Colorful Morning Glory Pool in Yellowstone National Park

Bisons in the fumaroles of Black Sand Basin in winter, Yellowstone National Park

Physical Systems

Ring of Fire

The Ring of Fire is a horseshoe-shaped area around the Pacific Ocean. Many volcanic eruptions have occurred in the Ring of Fire. Some of the most active countries in the Ring of Fire are Japan, Indonesia, Mexico, Chile, Guatemala, New Zealand, the Philippines, and Ecuador. These places are known for their frequent volcanic activity.

The Ring of Fire was created by tectonic plates, or huge slabs of solid rock, moving like giant rafts on the Earth's surface. These plates sometimes slide next to, collide with, and are forced underneath each other. The Pacific Plate and the surrounding plates do this often, causing earthquakes. When the plates collide, this also creates a huge amount of energy. The energy melts rocks into magma, or hot, molten rock. This magma then rises to the surface as lava and forms volcanoes. There are more than 450 volcanoes along the Ring of Fire.

Answer the items.

1. What is the difference between an earthquake and a volcano?

_____

_____

2. Which would you be more afraid of: an earthquake or a volcano?

_____

3. How close do you live to the Ring of Fire?

_____

Skill Sharpeners: Geography • EMC 3743 • © Evan-Moor Corp.

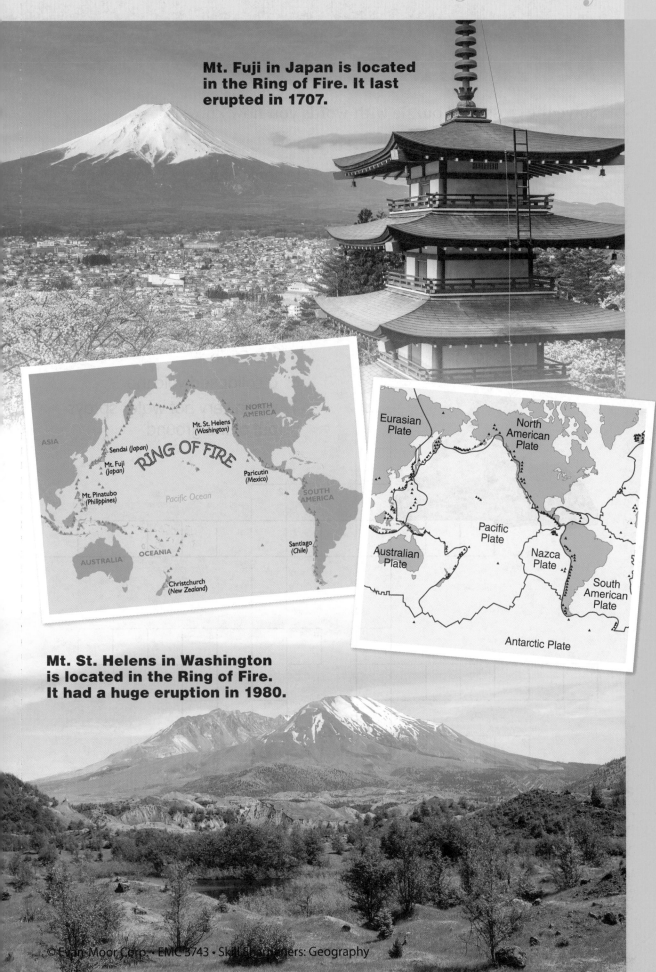

Mt. Fuji in Japan is located in the Ring of Fire. It last erupted in 1707.

ASIA

NORTH AMERICA

Mt. St. Helens (Washington)

Sendai (Japan)

RING OF FIRE

Mt. Fuji (Japan)

Paricutin (Mexico)

Mt. Pinatubo (Philippines)

Pacific Ocean

SOUTH AMERICA

Santiago (Chile)

AUSTRALIA

OCEANIA

Christchurch (New Zealand)

Eurasian Plate

North American Plate

Pacific Plate

Australian Plate

Nazca Plate

South American Plate

Antarctic Plate

Mt. St. Helens in Washington is located in the Ring of Fire. It had a huge eruption in 1980.

Physical Systems

Skill:
Apply content
vocabulary

Active Earth

Solve the crossword puzzle with words you now know!

| caldera | ring of fire | tectonic plate | core |
| volcano | geyser | earthquake | |

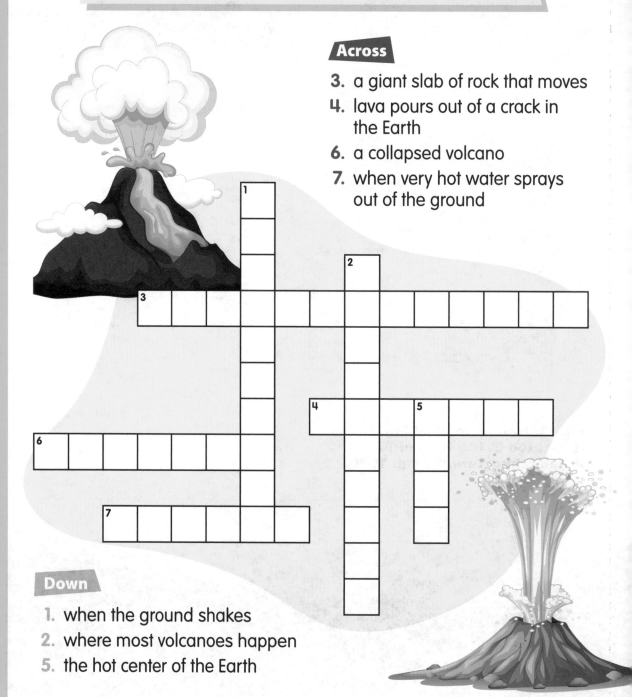

Across

3. a giant slab of rock that moves
4. lava pours out of a crack in the Earth
6. a collapsed volcano
7. when very hot water sprays out of the ground

Down

1. when the ground shakes
2. where most volcanoes happen
5. the hot center of the Earth

Physical Systems

Skill:
Apply geography concepts in context

Eruption!

In this activity, you will make a miniature volcano erupt.

What You Need

- tray
- 16-ounce plastic cup
- spoon
- water
- 4 to 6 tablespoons baking soda
- 1 teaspoon dish soap
- 1 ounce washable red paint
- 1 cup (8 ounces) vinegar
- dirt

What You Do

1. Pour water into the cup until it is two-thirds full.

2. Add in the baking soda, dish soap, and paint.

3. Stir the ingredients.

4. On the tray, make a cone-shaped volcano with the dirt until it is about 1 foot (30 cm) high.

5. Dig a hole at the top of the volcano just big enough to hold the cup.

6. Place the cup in the hole. Pat the dirt close to the cup's rim.

7. Pour the vinegar into the mixture and watch the eruption!

Physical Systems

Skill:
Write informative text to convey information and experiences clearly

A Trip to Yellowstone!

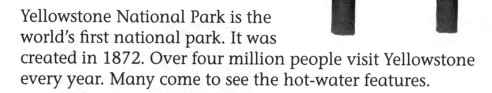

Yellowstone National Park is the world's first national park. It was created in 1872. Over four million people visit Yellowstone every year. Many come to see the hot-water features.

Write to tell what features you would like to see at Yellowstone National Park. Explain what you think it will be like to see the features in person.

_____

_____

_____

_____

_____

_____

_____

_____

_____

_____

_____

_____

Physical Systems

Mistake in the Desert

Concept:
Different biomes exist on Earth's surface.

My parents once made a mistake on our vacation. One summer we decided to take a grand tour of several national parks. One of those places was Death Valley in California.

Death Valley is the lowest place in North America. Its elevation at one spot is 282 feet (86 m) below sea level. One day the temperature reached 134°F (57°C). That is the world's hottest temperature ever recorded!

It was July, midsummer, when we were there. We were standing at a view point and could see heat shimmering off the rocks and road. Nothing seemed to be moving or alive. There was rock, dirt, hills, mountains, and sand dunes, but no wind and hardly any plants. The car thermometer read 125°F (52°C) as we stood outside guzzling the last of our water.

Dad said, "Now we know why this valley got its name. There's not much alive out here." Then Mom added, "Actually, the name comes from some miners who tried to cross the valley in the 1800s and didn't make it."

Either way, Death Valley is a hot, dry desert. Our mistake was coming there in summer. We quickly left our view point and drove to a small store. We all bought bottles of cold water, had an ice-cream cone, and got back into our car to head for the mountains.

Physical Systems

Concept:
Different biomes exist on Earth's surface.

Deserts All Over the World

Define It!

desert: a hot or cold place with little precipitation

precipitation: rain, hail, sleet, or snow

evaporation: water disappearing into the air

Death Valley is part of the Mojave and Colorado Deserts of North America. Deserts are places on Earth that get very little precipitation. Deserts also have more evaporation than rain or snow. That means what little water they get quickly disappears into the air. There are deserts all over the world, and most of them are hot like Death Valley. But there are cold deserts, too, including the Arctic and Antarctica.

The largest hot desert is the Sahara. It is on the continent of Africa. The Sahara is huge—about the size of China and the United States put together. The Sahara is known for having vast areas of endless sand dunes blowing in the wind.

A large part of Australia is desert. Most of the western part of the country is incredibly dry. There are some scattered small towns and cities in the desert of Australia, which some people call the Outback.

The Atacama Desert of Chile is the driest desert in the world. It is so dry that some parts of it have never seen a drop of rain. In other parts of the Atacama, people have said the rocky soil and lack of plants make it look like Mars.

Answer the items.

1. Do you want to visit a desert? Why or why not?

_____

_____

2. How do you think you would feel while walking in the Sahara Desert?

_____

Physical Systems

Death Valley National Park, California

Sand dunes in the Sahara Desert, Morocco, Africa

Moon Valley, Atacama Desert, Chile

The Australian Outback, South Australia

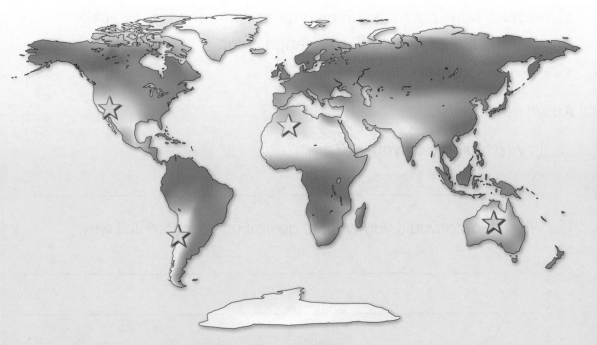

Physical Systems

Concept:
Different biomes exist on Earth's surface.

Biomes All Over the World

Define It!

biome: an area of plants, animals, and insects that live and work together

tundra: a cold, frozen area with tiny plants

taiga: a cold, moist forested area

Deserts are one type of biome on Earth. A biome is where all living things in that area—the plants, animals, and insects—work together as a community.

Another type of biome is a grassland. This is a large area with small plants, shrubs, and grasses. It is too wet to be a desert and too dry for trees. This is also sometimes called a savanna.

Tundra is another biome. This is a mostly cold area with only tiny plants. Most of the year, tundra is covered in snow and ice. There are no trees because the weather is far too cold. Tundra occurs toward the North Pole or on the peaks of high, cold mountains.

Forests are another type of biome. A tropical rainforest has an incredible amount of living things in it. Tropical rainforests are also hot, humid, and rainy. Temperate rainforests have a warm season and a cool one. They also get a lot of rain and are thick with trees. Finally, there is the taiga forest. This area is moist and cold most of the year. Taiga plants, such as pine and fir trees, are typically evergreen, so their leaves don't change color.

Answer the items.

1. In which biome do you live?

_____

2. Which biome would you want to go visit on vacation? Tell why.

_____

Physical Systems

Kenya Masai Mara Park savanna in Africa ☆

A vast tundra in the Arctic ☆

Siberian coniferous taiga, Sayan Mountains in Russia ☆

Sol Duc Rainforest at Olympic National Park in Washington State ☆

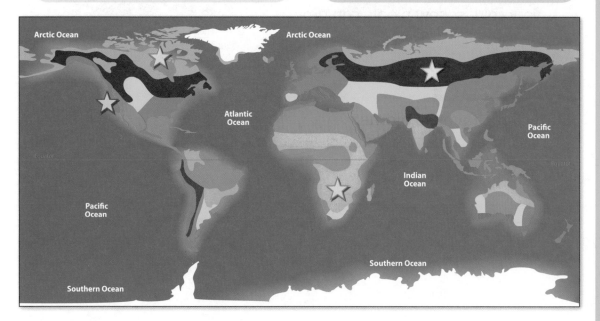

⬜ Ice sheet and polar desert	🟦 Mixed and deciduous forest	🟨 Savanna
🟩 Tundra	🟩 Tropical rainforest	🟥 Desert
⬛ Taiga	🟩 Steppe	🟥 Mediterranean vegetation
🟫 Montane (alpine tundra and montane forest)		

Physical Systems

Skill:
Apply content vocabulary in context

The World's Biomes

Match the word or words to its description.

taiga	tropical rainforest	savanna	precipitation
tundra	temperate rainforest	desert	

1. a forested area that is cold and moist _____

2. an area of mostly grasses and some shrubs _____

3. warm, rainy, and lots of plants and animals _____

4. rainy with seasons, lots of trees _____

5. rain, hail, sleet, or snow _____

6. a place that gets little rain _____

7. very cold, so few plants can grow _____

Think About It

Draw your favorite biome.

Desert at Your House?

Skill:
Apply geography concepts in context

In this activity, you will explore outside around your house to find out what locations are warmer than others.

What You Need

- thermometers
- paper
- pencil

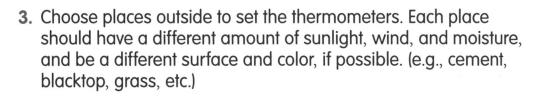

What You Do

1. Gather as many thermometers as you can.

2. Make sure you know how to read the thermometers for the current temperature.

3. Choose places outside to set the thermometers. Each place should have a different amount of sunlight, wind, and moisture, and be a different surface and color, if possible. (e.g., cement, blacktop, grass, etc.)

4. Place each thermometer and leave it there for 10 minutes to let the temperature settle.

5. After 10 minutes, record the temperature of each thermometer. Make sure that you look at the number before you pick up the thermometer or breathe on it. Handling the thermometer could change the temperature!

6. Compare the temperatures. Then answer the questions.

   Which place was warmest? _____

   Which place was coolest? _____

   Why do you think the temperatures were different in different locations? What location was most like a desert?

   _____

   _____

Physical Systems

Skill:
Write informative text to convey information and experiences clearly

Going to the Desert

Deserts are often hot and always dry. However, many people live in deserts. People also vacation in them to see their amazing scenery, plants, and animals.

Pretend you are going away to the desert. Write what you'd like to see and what you need to bring to make your journey safe and comfortable.

_____

_____

_____

_____

_____

_____

_____

_____

_____

_____

_____

_____

_____

Physical Systems

Skill Sharpeners: Geography • EMC 3743 • © Evan-Moor Corp.

Moving Day

Moving day was sad. I had known about it for months. My mom got a new job across the country and we sold our house. We loaded our things into the moving van and set off for California.

At first, we planned a week to get there. But Mom said we could each choose three places to visit along the way. We took out the map and decided what to see between New York and Los Angeles.

My mom chose to stop and see Niagara Falls. She also wanted to see the arch in St. Louis, Missouri, and the Grand Canyon in Arizona.

Me? I wanted to stop and see a Chicago Cubs game. I'm in Little League and my team is the Cubs. After that, I wanted to see Mt. Rushmore in South Dakota. My last stop was Dinosaur National Monument in Utah. We had a lot to look forward to. Our journey ended up taking ten days with all the zigzagging around.

When we finally got to Los Angeles and unpacked, my mom said, "Everyone will come visit us now. There's so much to see here." I hope she is right, but on the first day of school I made a new friend. So I guess it wasn't so bad.

Concept:
People move to different locations for a variety of reasons.

Human Systems

Concept:
People move to different locations for a variety of reasons.

Going to California

Define It!

Gold Rush: the period of time when many people came to California hoping to find gold

population: the number of people living in an area

industry: all the businesses that make or do a particular type of thing

People have been moving to California for a long time! It started with the Gold Rush in the mid-1800s. Miners went there to try and strike it rich in the goldfields. Other people went to California to start businesses or provide services to the miners.

In the 1900s, California's population continued to grow. The fertile San Joaquin Valley of California became, and still is, one of the most important farming regions in the world. Industry, or the making of goods and services, is also well known in California. One of those industries is moviemaking. In the 1920s and '30s, Hollywood in Southern California became the film center of the world. Many movies were made there. Some of the movies showed the California lifestyle, which included sunny beaches, warm mountain hikes, and happy people at Disneyland. Those movies inspired even more people to move to California.

The computer industry's boom started in the 1980s and '90s in an area south of San Francisco called Silicon Valley. It was named after the silicon chips used in computers. Today, California has a population of over 39 million people, making it the most populated state in the United States.

Answer the items.

1. What question do you have about the state of California?

   _____

   _____

2. Would you want to live in California? Why or why not?

   _____

Skill Sharpeners: Geography • EMC 3743 • © Evan-Moor Corp.

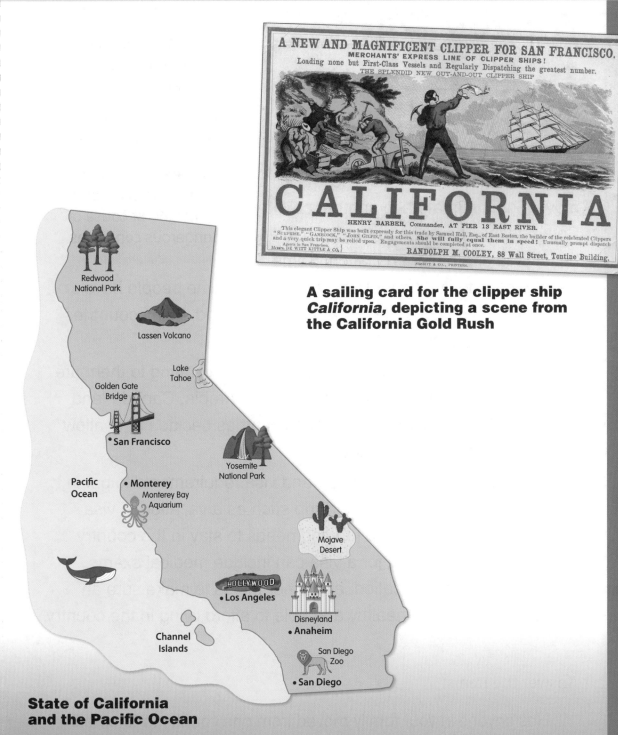

A sailing card for the clipper ship *California,* depicting a scene from the California Gold Rush

State of California and the Pacific Ocean

Human Systems

A New Place to Call Home

Define It!

migrant: a person who moves from one place to another

immigrant: a person who moves to another country

refugee: a person forced to move from his or her homeland because of dangerous conditions

The world has over 7 billion people living in it. Over 200 million of these people are called migrants. They have moved, or immigrated, to another country. Some people leave their homeland to find better jobs or a better education. Some people move to find better living conditions. Some people have to leave their home because of wars or lack of food. Many countries help these refugees.

The countries that have the most people migrating to them are the United States, Russia, Germany, Saudi Arabia, Canada, and the United Kingdom. But sometimes countries decide not to allow many people to enter their country.

Countries also have passport and visa requirements to get in. A passport is needed for a short trip such as a vacation. A visa is needed if a person has a job and needs to stay in the country for many years. Applying for a visa can include medical exams, vaccination forms, education, and other things to make sure an immigrating person is healthy and able to afford living in the country.

Answer the items.

1. Has anyone in your family moved from one country to another? What was the reason?

   _____

2. Do you have a passport? If so, which countries have you visited?

   _____

U.S. immigration forms

A Cuban immigration office in Santa Clara, Cuba

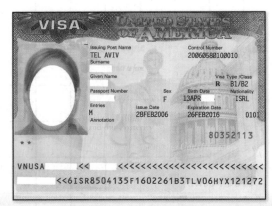

A visitor's visa to the United States of America

Syrian refugee families who came from Kobani District living in tents in the Suruc District of Sanliurfa, Turkey

Human Systems

Moving to a New Country

Solve this crossword puzzle about people moving to a new country.

| migrant | industry | population | visa |
| immigrate | refugee | gold rush | |

Across

1. the number of people that live in an area
4. all businesses that make or provide things for others
6. a time when many people came to California to seek gold
7. a person who moves from place to place

Down

2. when someone moves to a new country
3. a permit needed to stay in a country for a long period of time
5. someone forced to escape from a country with dangerous conditions

Human Systems

Skill Sharpeners: Geography • EMC 3743 • © Evan-Moor Corp.

Design a Passport

Imagine that you are going on a trip around the world. Make a passport and design stamps for the different countries you'd like to visit.

What You Need

- 1 sheet of white writing paper

- 1 sheet of colored construction paper

- your personal information: your name, gender, date of birth, place of birth, and nationality

- a photo of yourself

- pencil, ruler, and colored pencils/markers

- scissors and glue

- computer with Internet access

What You Do

1. Fold the sheet of writing paper in half horizontally. Then fold it in half vertically. Trim the bottom edge of the folded paper so it makes four pages.

2. Fold the construction paper in half to make a cover for the pages. Put the pages inside the cover. Cut the cover to fit. Staple the middle fold of the pages and the cover together. This is your "passport" booklet.

3. Use the Internet to research what various passports look like. (Select "images" in the search results.) Also research what passport stamps issued by different countries look like.

4. Decorate your passport cover. Glue your photo on the first page of the booklet and write your personal information (listed above) below it.

5. On the inside pages of your booklet, draw the passport stamps from all of the countries you'd like to visit.

Human Systems

Skill:
Write narrative text about real-world situations

Time to Move!

Pretend you have to immigrate to another country. How would you feel about moving? What would you bring with you? What would you have to leave behind?

Write about the country you are moving to and what you think life will be like.

_____

_____

_____

_____

_____

_____

_____

_____

_____

_____

_____

_____

Human Systems

Skill Sharpeners: Geography • EMC 3743 • © Evan-Moor Corp.

My Bilingual Education

Concept:
Spoken and written languages are distinctive characteristics of a culture.

My parents put me in a bilingual classroom starting in first grade. I am in third grade now. We spoke English at home until I started learning Spanish. Now I say a few words to my parents in Spanish every day so they can learn a second language, too. My parents say it is easier to learn a second language when you are young, and that is why they wanted me to learn it early. I think it's a good idea, too, because there are many Spanish-speaking people where I live in California.

The class I'm in speaks English for half of the day and Spanish for the other half. In California, the second most common language spoken is Spanish. I am getting better and better at speaking Spanish every year.

Now, when my third-grade teacher says things like, "Bien, clase. Por favor saquen el libro de lectura," I know that means, "Okay class, it is time to take out your reading book."

I used to have a lot of trouble understanding directions when my teacher started speaking in Spanish. Sometimes I would look around the class to see what others were doing before I knew what to do. But I am getting better at it. My parents say if I keep learning Spanish, I will have a better chance of getting a job when I am an adult because I speak two languages.

Hola – Hello

Por favor – Please

Bienvenido – You are welcome

Gracias – Thank you

Human Systems

Concept:

Spoken and written languages are distinctive characteristics of a culture.

Four Languages in One Country!

Switzerland is a small country right in the middle of Europe. Over 8 million people live there. Switzerland is surrounded by much larger and more populated countries on all sides. There is Germany to the north, Italy to the south, Austria to the east, and France to the west. Because of its location and history, there are four official languages in the country of Switzerland.

The most common language in Switzerland is Swiss German. The second most common is Swiss French, and the third is Swiss Italian. A small number of people in Switzerland still speak an ancient language called Romansch. Each of the three main languages is a special dialect. That means it is different from the traditional native language spoken in the neighboring country. The language is its own Swiss version of the original language. Also, most people in Switzerland speak and understand some English. The dominant, or most spoken, language of each region in Switzerland depends on its proximity, or location, to the country surrounding it. Most children going to school in Switzerland speak and learn several languages at the same time.

Answer the items.

1. If you lived in Switzerland, what languages would you like to speak?

   _____

   _____

2. Do you think it is better to learn one language at a time or more than one?

   _____

   _____

Human Systems

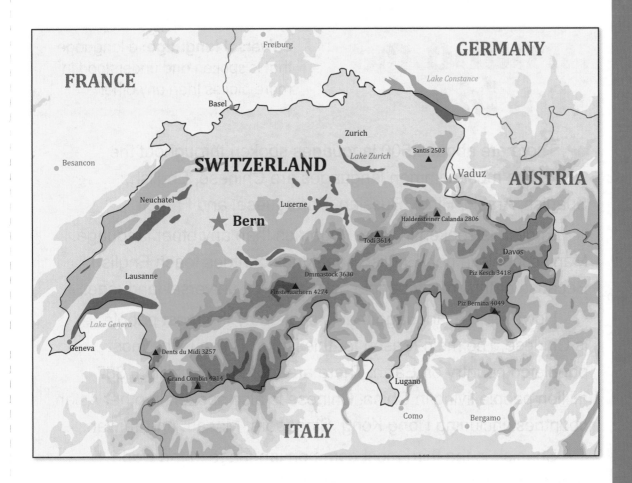

FRANCE

GERMANY

Freiburg

Lake Constance

Basel

Besancon

SWITZERLAND

Zurich

Lake Zurich

Santis 2503

Vaduz

AUSTRIA

Neuchatel

Lucerne

★ Bern

Haldensteiner Calanda 2806

Todi 3614

Davos

Lausanne

Dmmastock 3630

Piz Kesch 3418

Finsteraarhorn 4274

Piz Bernina 4049

Lake Geneva

Geneva

Dents du Midi 3257

Grand Combin 4314

Lugano

Como

Bergamo

ITALY

Zurich City Center surrounds River Limmat in Switzerland

Human Systems

Concept:

Spoken and written languages are distinctive characteristics of a culture.

Languages Around the World

Define It!

universal language: a language that is spoken and understood in more places than any other

There are about 6,500 languages spoken throughout the world. The most common languages are Chinese, English, Spanish, Arabic, Hindi, Russian, Portuguese, and French.

English is spoken in more countries than any other language. Many schools in non-English-speaking countries teach English. Because of this, many people call English a universal language.

However, the language that is spoken by the most people is Chinese. The main reason for this is that China is the most populated country on Earth. There are more than 1 billion, 387 million people living in China. Chinese is also spoken in other Asian countries, including Hong Kong, Singapore, Macau, and Taiwan.

Spanish is the third most common language in the world. It is spoken in Spain and Mexico. Spanish is also spoken in many countries of Central and South America, including Costa Rica, Guatemala, Honduras, Chile, and Peru.

Answer the items.

1. What language besides English might be called a universal language?

   _____

2. Which of the most common languages would you like to learn? Why?

   _____

   _____

Skill Sharpeners: Geography • EMC 3743 • © Evan-Moor Corp.

Locals and tourists in downtown Shanghai, China

Tourists in downtown Mercat Central (Mercado Central or Central Market) Square in Valencia, Spain

Human Systems

Skill:
Use visual
discrimination

Many Languages

Find these language-related words in the word search.
Hint: Some are backwards.

dialect	proximity	switzerland	chinese
english	spanish	native	universal

s	s	n	o	e	s	s	a	m	p	f	e	z	j	q
c	w	y	v	g	p	h	u	r	r	y	s	c	n	u
t	w	i	y	q	s	x	p	s	o	o	e	p	d	b
s	c	u	t	i	w	o	p	a	x	p	n	b	e	q
l	y	e	l	z	k	m	j	z	i	i	i	q	d	g
e	r	g	l	t	e	g	n	u	m	q	h	z	n	g
c	n	x	e	a	g	r	n	l	i	d	c	z	p	m
e	a	l	y	i	i	i	l	d	t	l	e	j	c	r
h	q	n	w	p	v	d	m	a	y	i	v	x	f	g
y	l	j	o	e	u	s	p	a	n	i	s	h	p	x
f	i	a	r	w	w	v	c	d	t	d	m	p	o	b
b	m	s	g	g	x	b	g	c	b	o	f	l	v	k
o	a	r	h	n	a	t	i	v	e	s	n	l	t	h
l	y	y	h	t	n	p	f	g	f	y	f	p	j	g
h	o	c	l	w	u	b	v	z	t	l	h	c	a	a

Hello Around the World

Learn how to say "hello" in different languages!

Language	Word	Pronunciation	Meaning
French	bonjour	bohn-ZHUR	"good day" or "good morning"
Spanish	hola	O-lah	"hello"
Arabic	marhaba	mar-HAH-bah	"hello" or "welcome"
Hindi	namaste	nah-mah-STAY	"hello" or "goodbye"
Mandarin	ni hao	NEE-how	"hello"
Pashto	salaam	sah-LAHM	"hello" or "goodbye"

What You Do

1. Use the chart to practice greeting people in different languages. Ask an adult to help you.

2. Research other words or phrases from one of the languages above or a language of your choosing.

Human Systems

Skill:
Write narrative text about real-world situations

Juggling Languages

Write a story about a boy or girl who moves to a new school and does not speak the same language as everyone else. Tell about how the kids at school treat him or her.

_____

_____

_____

_____

_____

_____

_____

_____

_____

_____

Human Systems

Skill Sharpeners: Geography • EMC 3743 • © Evan-Moor Corp.

Cliff Palace

One year my parents took me to visit Mesa Verde National Park in Colorado. The ranger led us down a series of steep steps into the Cliff Palace Ruin. This is the biggest ancient living area at Mesa Verde and in North America. Cliff Palace was full of rooms made of mortar, or a combination of mud, water, and ash. The Ancestral Puebloans who once lived there also used sandstone and wood beams to make their homes.

There were dozens of these old homes at Cliff Palace. Also scattered in the Cliff Palace area were several kivas. Kivas go below the ground. Ancestral Puebloans had their religious ceremonies in kivas, which are similar to churches or synagogues for people today.

We followed the ranger down into a kiva. There was a hole in the floor of the kiva that looked like a fire pit. The ranger told us that it is a sípapu, or place of emergence. That is where Hopi people believed they emerged from a previous world into this one.

As I sat in the kiva, I imagined how the Ancestral Puebloans lived and what they believed. It kind of gave me the chills to know I was standing where they stood. I wondered why the Puebloans left. I have a lot of unanswered questions, but I will always remember my visit to Mesa Verde as a magical experience.

Human Systems

Green Table

Concept:
Settlements are established where locations provide opportunities.

Mesa Verde National Park is in southwest Colorado in the United States. It was established on June 29, 1906. Much of the park sits high up on flat mountains that turn green in the summer due to thunderstorms. The park is mostly known for the ancient homes, or archaeological sites, of the Ancestral Puebloans. An archaeological site is a location with historical homes, artifacts, or ruins. The homes at Mesa Verde are some of the best preserved in the entire world.

At Mesa Verde there are about 5,000 of these sites, including 600 cliff dwellings, which are the homes the people lived in from AD 1200 to AD 1300. Rangers offer guided tours of many of the ruins all summer long.

For a long time it was a mystery why the people who once lived there left. Experts now believe that a drought forced them to move elsewhere. The Puebloan people could not grow their crops in drought conditions, so they probably left and searched for a new place that had more rainfall.

Answer the items.

1. Why is Mesa Verde called a "green table"?

_____

2. Why do you think many of the tours at Mesa Verde are guided by rangers?

_____

_____

3. If you could ask the Puebloans a question, what would you ask them?

_____

Human Systems

View of the Spruce Tree House in Mesa Verde National Park, Colorado

Ladder descending into a kiva in Mesa Verde National Park, Colorado

Cliff Palace in Mesa Verde National Park, Colorado

Human Systems

Human Systems

Inca Royalty

High up in the Andes Mountains of Peru lies the ancient city of Machu Picchu. Machu Picchu is at nearly 8,000 feet (2,438 m) elevation on a mountain plateau. A plateau is a flat area near the top of a mountain.

Define It!

sanctuary: a special place for religious leaders and others

abandoned: to be left behind and forgotten about

artifact: an ancient object made by humans

Built in the 1400s, Machu Picchu was once a sanctuary, or special religious place, for Inca leaders. The city had over 150 buildings, some of which were homes, bath houses, and temples. These buildings were originally constructed with dry stone walls. In the 1500s, about 100 years after it was built, the Incas were scared away by the conquering Spanish civilization. The Incas left and the city was abandoned.

Machu Picchu was unknown to the world until 1911. In 1911, an American archaeologist stumbled upon the ruins of the lost city. An archaeologist is a person who studies ancient civilizations and their artifacts. By the 1900s, much of the city had been overgrown by the thick, jungle-like plants. And many of the buildings were in disrepair, or broken down. Now Machu Picchu is being reconstructed, or built just like it used to be. Over a million people from all over visit it yearly to see one of the world's most famous man-made wonders.

Answer the items.

1. Why do you think Machu Picchu was built high in the mountains?

   _____

2. Why do you think nobody knew about Machu Picchu for about 350 years?

   _____

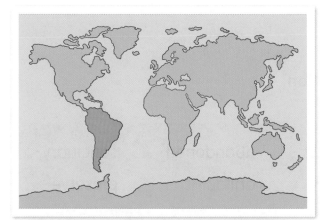

Machu Picchu

South America

Machu Picchu, the ancient Incan city in the Andes, Peru

Intihuatana at Machu Picchu in Peru

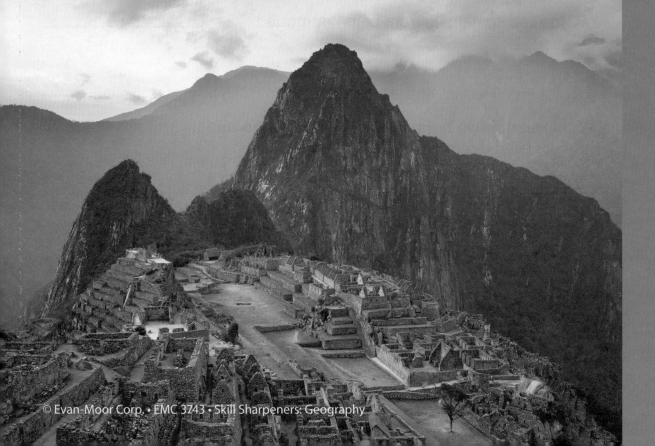

Human Systems

Skill:
Apply content vocabulary in context

Ancient Sites

Write the word next to its definition.

| drought | archaeologist | abandoned | sanctuary |
| Mesa Verde | ruins | artifact | preserve |

1. "green table" in Spanish _____

2. a person who studies the past and its artifacts _____

3. an item created by people long ago _____

4. a special religious place _____

5. the ancient remains of something _____

6. a period of very dry weather _____

7. to be left behind and forgotten about _____

8. to keep something from being damaged _____

Think About It

What might have happened if Machu Picchu and its artifacts had *not* been discovered?

_____

_____

_____

_____

Human Systems

Skill Sharpeners: Geography • EMC 3743 • © Evan-Moor Corp.

Uncovering Artifacts

Skill:
Apply geography concepts in real-world situations

Bury artifacts in your backyard and have someone find them!

What You Need

- 5 "artifacts" from your home
- paintbrush
- outdoor area with sand or dirt
- tray to place items on
- small shovel
- water

What You Do

1. Find several items inside your house that are old, small, and not too fragile. Ask your parents if you can use the items. Be sure to tell them they will get dirty.

2. After gathering the items, find a sand or dirt area in your yard where you can bury them as artifacts.

3. Invite a friend or family member to carefully dig out the items just like an archaeologist would. Tell him or her that the items are old and from an ancient civilization.

4. After the items have been dug out, clean them with water or the dry paintbrush. Place them on the tray for further display and inspection.

5. Describe the items as if you are an archaeologist. Provide the following facts:
   - What are they?
   - How old are they?
   - What were they used for?
   - Who used them?

Human Systems

Skill:
Write narrative
text about real-
world situations

Clues to the Past

Artifacts and ruins are clues to the past. How could studying these help tell us what a place was like when it was full of people? Pretend that you are an archaeologist and you have dug up some artifacts. Write about what you found and who you think the items belonged to.

_____

_____

_____

_____

_____

_____

_____

_____

_____

_____

_____

_____

Human Systems

Read the News

We all got out of the car just outside of Canyonlands National Park in Utah. My mom said to my sister and I, "You two read the newspaper, right?" "Sometimes," I replied. Mom asked, "How would you like to read a newspaper that is over one thousand years old?"

I was confused. How would it last that long? Was paper even invented back then? Would I even be able to read it now?

Mom led our family over to a large slab of rock. A sign in front called it Newspaper Rock. Immediately, I knew why. There were hundreds of pieces of rock art etched all over the rock. Some were life-sized or even larger. I saw animals that looked like deer, buffalo, and pronghorn. I also saw what appeared to be people riding a horse. There were other mysterious drawings and symbols as well. Mom said, "These are petroglyphs, or carvings in the rock, done by native peoples."

Petroglyphs on Newspaper Rock near Canyonlands National Park, Utah

The sign also said that some of the carvings were up to 2,000 years old. They were made by several different native groups who used to live in the area. I also learned that the rock is called Tse Hone, which means "Rock that tells a story." We all gazed at the amazing rock art in awe, wondering what it all meant.

Human Systems

X-ray Art

Concept:
Cultures leave imprints on the physical environment.

Define It!

Aboriginals: native people of Australia

ocher: a natural substance found in clay soil used for painting

organs: internal body parts such as the heart and liver

In Northern Australia there is a national park called Kakadu. There are many spectacular features at Kakadu. One of them has some of the oldest and best-known rock art in the world.

Native Aboriginals have lived at Kakadu for up to 40,000 years. Over the years, they have left behind rock art, shelters, stone tools, grindstones, and ceremonial ocher. Ocher is a substance found in the earth used for painting. It is one of Earth's oldest paints. Kakadu's rock art is special because it is up to 20,000 years old. But it is also amazing because of the subjects painted. Kakadu rock art has very unusual "x-ray art." Aboriginals, or native people of Australia, painted bones and internal organs of animals such as the heart, lungs, and liver. Kakadu rock art also has paintings of spirits and healers.

Rock art at Kakadu shows the tools Aboriginals used, the animals they hunted, and the activities they did. Many animal paintings were meant to show a successful hunt. There are also many types of fish shown in the rock art. Some of the rock art is about how Aboriginals see the creation of the world.

Today, rock art at Kakadu is mostly done on bark, paper, canvas, and fabric instead of rocks. This makes Kakadu one of the longest periods of rock art displays that can be seen in the world.

Answer the items.

1. What is "x-ray art"?

_____

2. What can you think of to use as a natural paint?

Human Systems

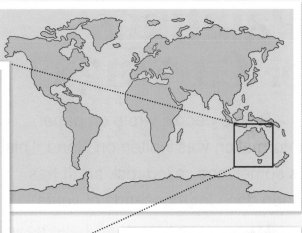

Australia

Kakadu
National Park

Ancient mineral - bright ocher stones and powder used as natural color paint pigment

Aboriginal rock art in Kakadu National Park, Northern Territory, Australia

Human Systems

Paintings or Carvings?

Before people wrote on paper, information was written on stone. This is sometimes called rock art. It has been done for thousands of years.

Many areas of rock art have been worn away by the elements. In caves and protected areas, rock art panels last longer. Also, areas with an arid, or very dry, climate have longer-lasting rock art.

The two types of rock art are petroglyphs and pictographs. A petroglyph is when art is carved into the rock. This can be done by scratching away the rock's surface, or by carving an indentation, or groove, into the rock. The other method is a pictograph. Pictographs are when pigments or minerals, including charcoal from a fire pit, are used to paint art. Pictographs tend not to be as durable, or long-lasting, because they can be washed off.

Each method was used for different reasons. If there was a "paint" or natural substance available, that was used. If the rock was soft enough to be scratched or etched in to, this method was used. There are rock art panels found all over the world that use both methods.

Answer the items.

1. What causes rock art to be worn away?

   _____

2. Why does rock art in caves last longer?

   _____

The "Holy Ghost and Companions" are life-sized pictographs in Horseshoe Canyon, Utah.

Newspaper Rock is a large cliff mural of ancient petroglyphs. Images were made by Native Americans during both the prehistoric and historic periods.

Newspaper Rock State Historic Monument is in Utah.

Skill:
Identify content
vocabulary

Rock Art

Draw a line from the definition to its word.

1. very dry weather with little rain •

• elements

2. internal body parts such as the heart •

• arid

3. a mineral or element in the soil used for making paint •

• petroglyph

4. original people of the Australian continent •

• pictograph

5. weather events such as wind and rain that occur naturally •

• Aboriginals

6. rock art created with paint •

• ocher

7. rock art that is scratched or carved •

• organs

Think About It

Rock art was meant to last for a long time. If you were to create rock art, what message would you want to share with future generations? Explain your answer.

_____

_____

_____

_____

_____

Human Systems

Skill Sharpeners: Geography • EMC 3743 • © Evan-Moor Corp.

Skill:
Apply geography concepts in real-world situations

Become a Rock Artist

Make rock art by painting or scratching on a real rock.

What You Need

- paints or food coloring of various colors OR paints from foods such as blueberries, beets, strawberries, or cherries

- light-colored flat rocks to paint on and/or sharp rocks to use to scratch pictures onto another rock

- paintbrushes   • gloves and safety goggles (or glasses)

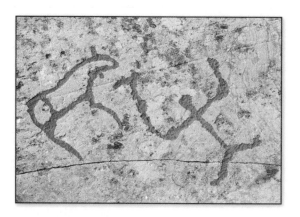 

What You Do

1. Decide if your rock art will be painted on or scratched on or both.

2. Depending on how you decide to create your rock art, find flat rocks to paint on or sharp rocks to scratch the flat rocks with.

3. If you are using paints from foods, prepare them by cutting the food into small pieces. Then crush the pieces with the back of a spoon until you have made a thin paste.

4. Copy one of the rock art drawings shown above or create your own rock art.

5. Show your finished rock art to your family.

Human Systems

Skill:
Write informative text to convey information and experiences clearly

Preserving the Past

Panels of rock art are clues to the past. They are very fragile and can be easily destroyed just by the oils on our skin. Pretend you have just discovered a new panel of rock art, unknown to the world until now. Write about what you would do to protect it. Then tell how you would make sure it was preserved for future generations.

_____

_____

_____

_____

_____

_____

_____

_____

_____

_____

_____

_____

_____

_____

Human Systems

Skill Sharpeners: Geography • EMC 3743 • © Evan-Moor Corp.

A Lake by Mistake

Concept:
People use technology to get what they need from the physical environment.

If I could go back in time, I would choose to see some incredible events. One would be the making of the Salton Sea in California. This lake was made completely by mistake during the years 1905 to 1907.

Millions of years ago, the Salton Sea was connected to the Pacific Ocean. But sediment, or dirt, from the Colorado River piled up and cut off the ocean. That left behind a very salty body of water. Because the area is in an arid desert, the inland sea eventually dried up.

It stayed that way until 1905. That's when people tried to divert, or change, where the water from the Colorado River flowed. People wanted it to flow into the extremely dry desert of southeastern California in order to water crops. The Colorado River comes from the snowy mountains of Colorado. But there was so much water in the river that year that it broke through the canals and started filling in the sea. For two years, water flooded over the buildings and salt mines that were there. By 1907, the Salton Sea was filled with water for the first time in millions of years. It is still there now, a vast inland sea with very salty and polluted water.

Environment and Society

The Bread Basket

Environment and Society

California, located in the western region of the United States, has been called the Bread Basket of the Earth. The state is the fifth-largest food supplier in the world. Over 400 crops are grown in California, including rice, dairy, grapes, almonds, walnuts, and many other types of fruits and vegetables. California's climate is good for growing food in some places, but not as good in others. Some parts of the state get a lot of rain and some get a lot of snow. Some parts get smaller amounts of precipitation. In some places, it hardly rains or snows at all.

The part of California where the most crops are grown is the San Joaquin and Sacramento Valleys. These areas have fertile soil perfect for growing crops, but much of the area is very dry. Dams have been built on rivers coming out of the mountains east of the valley. These dams have created large reservoirs, or water storage areas. Water is channeled out of reservoirs and aqueducts and travels through canals to water the crops. Moving water from one place to another for farming is called irrigation. If it weren't for California's irrigation system, the state would not be able to grow as many crops.

Define It!

climate: the weather in an area over a long period of time

precipitation: rain, hail, sleet, or snow

reservoir: a dammed up area created for storing water

aqueduct: a waterway to move water over or around an obstacle

canal: a man-made channel for moving water

Answer the items.

1. Is there a food you eat that comes from California? Tell what it is.

2. How do you think farmers in California feel about its irrigation system?

Water cascading over Lake Clementine Dam in Northern California

An irrigation canal distributing water to farms in the San Joaquin Valley, California

A potato field in the San Joaquin Valley using irrigation

Environment and Society

Concept:
People use technology to get what they need from the physical environment.

Moving Water

Define It!

irrigation: moving water from one place to another to water crops

shaduf: a device used for moving water from the river to a crop

canal: a man-made waterway to channel water through

Irrigation, or moving water from one place to another to water crops, has been done for a very long time. Ancient Egyptians used this method to grow their crops. Egypt is located within the Sahara Desert. This is the world's largest desert, and it is extremely dry there.

Long ago, Egypt's Nile River often flooded the Nile River valley. The floodwaters left behind rich soil, which was great for growing crops. But the area gets very little rain, so ancient Egyptians irrigated by carrying water from the river to the crops in bags made from the skin of animals. Sometimes shadufs were used to get water to the crops. A shaduf is a large bucket attached to a lever. This would allow farmers to scoop out water from the river and move it to their crops.

Later, Egyptians built dams on the river to increase water storage. From the dams, Egyptians moved water to their crops in canals. Other ancient civilizations, such as the Roman Empire, moved water from one place to another as well. And some of the Native Americans living in the desert of the southwest United States did, too.

Answer the item.

Think of another way the ancient Egyptians could have moved water. Write about it.

_____

_____

_____

Environment and Society

Mediterranean Sea

Egypt

Pyramids

Nile River

Illustration of Egyptian shadufs by an unidentified artist from Paris, circa 1842

Boats on the banks of the Nile, circa 1900

Sun rising above the Nile in Egypt

Environment and Society

Water Words

Solve this crossword puzzle about water and how people use it.

climate	reservoir	bread basket
shaduf	aqueduct	precipitation
dam	canal	irrigation

Across

1. man-made large storage area for water
4. wall to block and store water
6. channel for moving water long distances
7. weather patterns of an area
8. moving water from one place to another for crops
9. California's nickname

Down

2. bucket and lever for easier moving of water
3. rain, hail, sleet, or snow
5. channel for moving water around an obstacle

Skill Sharpeners: Geography • EMC 3743 • © Evan-Moor Corp.

Water Your Crops!

In your yard, create a miniature town with an irrigation system to water crops.

Skill:
Apply geography concepts in context

What You Need

- water
- straws
- sand or dirt
- blue food coloring
- plastic bags or plastic wrap for lining the sand

- trowel or small shovel
- bucket
- small toys or blocks to use as homes and crops

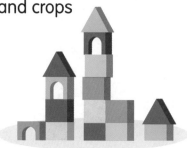

What You Do

1. Create a miniature town in the sand, using small toys or blocks as houses. Make one area of the town a field for growing crops. Find a place near the town to build a lake. The lake should be on higher ground than the town.

2. Dig a hole in the sand to make a lake. Line the lake with plastic bags or wrap to keep the water from soaking into the sand.

3. Use the bucket to fill the lake with water. Add a drop or two of blue food coloring.

4. Connect straws together so they reach from the lake to the field.

5. Pour water from the lake into the straws (if it will not flow on its own) to channel water to the field.

6. Show your irrigation system to someone and explain how it works.

Environment and Society

Environment and Society

Where Do You Get Your Water?

Where does the water in your town come from? Is there a storage area near you, such as a water tank or reservoir? How do you think water gets from where it is stored to your house? Ask an adult or do some research to find out the answers to these questions. Then draw a picture that shows how your town gets its water.

Parent Pampering

Concept:
The physical environment provides opportunities for human activities.

I have never seen my parents so relaxed! Let me tell you what made them feel that way.

We were in the middle of a long summer vacation. The plan was to visit as many United States national parks as we could. About one month into our trip, after we had visited dozens of parks, we stopped at a very unusual park. It was called Hot Springs National Park in the state of Arkansas. Like other parks we had visited, it had trails to hike, campgrounds, and picnic areas.

So what made this park so unusual? Hot springs! The springs are created from hot water that is thousands of feet underground. Thermal energy heats the water. People have been soaking in the hot pools for hundreds of years. The hot springs are said to heal the body. In fact, in the late 1800s, a row of bath houses was built so people could enjoy the hot springs in luxury. These heated pools and spas in the park use the thermal waters for special treatments such as baths and facials. My parents spent all day in the hot springs while I stayed with my sister and set up camp.

When my parents finally emerged from all their pampering, Mom said, "I feel so rejuvenated." Dad added, "I am going to sleep like a bear."

My sister and I? We were ready for a nice long hike!

Bath houses at Hot Springs in Arkansas, circa 1888

Environment and Society

Concept:
The physical environment provides opportunities for human activities.

New Zealand

In some places around the globe, hot springs are just the right temperature for people to bathe in. One of the most famous places for this is in New Zealand. New Zealand is highly volcanic. Because of that, water under the ground there is heated and comes back up to the surface. The temperature of that water ranges from warm to scalding hot.

New Zealand's most famous place for geothermal energy and hot water is the town of Rotorua. The area around Rotorua is in a large caldera. In and around Rotorua are hot pools and steam vents. There are also geysers that shoot hot water up to 100 feet (30 m) into the air. People from all over the world come to see these unusual hot-water features. Tourists, or people who vacation in and travel to different places, can stand under hot waterfalls, soak in mud pools, and enjoy spas using the hot water. There is one thing people have to put up with when visiting Rotorua, however. The hot water produces an unpleasant rotten egg, or sulphur, smell.

Answer the items.

1. Would you like to bathe in a hot spring? Tell why or why not.

   _____

   _____

2. Can you think of any reasons why geothermal energy could be dangerous?

   _____

   _____

Young woman enjoying a spa in an outdoor hot pool in Rotorua, New Zealand

Tourists watching erupting Lady Knox Geyser in the Wai-o-Tapu area of Rotorua, New Zealand

Sunset in the geothermal city of Rotorua, New Zealand

Environment and Society

Heat from the Ground

Define It!

fossil fuels: oil, coal, and gas used for heat and electricity

pollution: land, water, or air that is dirty or harmed

continental plates: huge slabs of rock that float on Earth's surface

Most places in the world get their electricity from fossils fuels. Fossil fuels are coal, oil, and gas. These fuels are not renewable, which means they will run out at some point. Using fossil fuels also causes pollution. Iceland does not use fossil fuels to produce most of their energy. Instead, most homes and businesses in Iceland use geothermal energy to heat their homes, get hot water, and generate, or make, electricity.

Iceland sits directly over a rift, or crack, in Earth's continental plates. That means the plates there are being pulled apart. This causes a large amount of volcanic activity below Iceland's ground. Also, Iceland gets a lot of rain and snow, which trickles underground and heats up.

In the early 1900s, the first Icelander learned how to use this energy to tap into the hot water. Now the government of Iceland has a whole system in place to use geothermal energy and deliver it to its people. There are five main geothermal energy plants in Iceland that do exactly this. Other countries are trying to learn from Iceland in order to use geothermal energy wherever they can, as well.

Answer the item.

Do you think it is a good idea to use geothermal energy instead of fossil fuels? Explain why or why not.

_____

_____

**Svartsengi geothermal
power station in Iceland**

**Geothermal power plant
in Bjarnarflag, Iceland**

**Hellisheidi geothermal
power plant in Iceland**

Strokkur Geyser erupting in Iceland

Environment and Society

Skill:
Apply geography concepts

Amazing Earth

Earth is an amazing place that provides many sights to see, resources to use, and natural places to enjoy. Read the description and write the word it describes.

caldera	geyser	tourists	geothermal
fossil fuels	hot spring	rift	continental plates

1. people who travel to different places _____

2. hot water that shoots out of the ground _____

3. oil, gas, and coal used for energy _____

4. a crack or split in the ground _____

5. a volcano that has collapsed _____

6. huge slabs of rock that float on Earth's surface _____

7. heat that comes from inside Earth _____

8. hot water that comes from underground _____

Think About It

Would you rather see a caldera or a geyser? Tell why.

_____

_____

_____

Environment and Society

Skill Sharpeners: Geography • EMC 3743 • © Evan-Moor Corp.

Moving Plates

Discover how plate movement shapes the land and forms mountains and volcanoes.

What You Need

- layered candy bars such as Snickers® or Milky Way®
- plastic knife
- plate

What You Do

1. Wash your hands. Unwrap the candy bar and place it on a plate.

2. Use the plastic knife to make cracks just in the chocolate, the outer layer of the candy bar.

3. Pretend the chocolate bar is the Earth's surface. The cracks show fault lines, or rifts, in the continental plates on Earth's surface.

4. Do the following things to simulate what happens to the Earth's surface:

   - Slowly pull the ends of the candy bar apart to create tension.

   - Slowly push the ends of the candy bar together to create compression.

   - Slowly slide the two halves of the candy bar in opposite directions, causing them to break apart.

5. All of these movements simulate what happens on Earth when plates collide, and landforms are made as a result. In addition, energy is formed where two plates collide, creating geothermal activity and volcanoes.

Environment and Society

You Found a Hot Spring!

Skill:
Write narrative text about real-world situations

Pretend you just discovered the most amazing hot spring. Thousands of people will want to come and sit in the healing waters, but the hot spring is hard to get to.

Write to tell how you would change the environment to make it ready for people to visit.

- What will you do to the environment around the hot spring so that people can come and enjoy it?
- Where will they stay after they get there?
- Will there be a place for them to buy food or a drink?

_____

_____

_____

_____

_____

_____

_____

_____

_____

Environment and Society

Gold Rush Days

Concept:
The location of resources affects patterns of settlement and trade.

I dipped my pan into the water. I lowered it far enough so a pile of sand and silt from the bottom of the stream filled the pan. I mixed in water and began swirling the pan around. Some of the water and light materials—rocks and sand—slipped over the edge of the pan and back into the stream. I swirled a little faster, hoping to speed things up. Some more water mixed with pebbles and sand fell over the sides and back into the water. All the time, I watched the pan and what was left in it, hoping to strike it rich.

A person dressed as a miner came up to me and explained, "The technique is to go slowly. Be patient. The lighter material will fall out, allowing the heavy stuff to settle at the bottom of the pan. That's the gold," he said. "Don't go too quickly!"

I took the miner's advice and slowed down, letting things fall out of the pan as slowly as I could. But I was still very impatient! Finally, nearing the end, there was just a little sand and pebbles left in my pan. As I slowly swirled around what remained, I saw it—a tiny fleck of gold! I picked up a pair of tweezers and plucked the prize out of the water and dropped it into my little glass vial. "I'm rich!" I announced. Everyone at the Gold Rush Days event looked at me and cheered.

Environment and Society

Concept:
The location of resources affects patterns of settlement and trade.

Finding Gold

Define It!

panning: using a pan with water to sift through dirt, soil, and rocks to find gold

hydraulic mining: spraying a high-powered hose at a hillside to loosen dirt to help find gold

sieves: containers with lots of small holes, used for separating large pieces from small pieces

There are several ways miners get gold out of the ground. The most popular way is probably panning. A person sifts and swirls small amounts of water, dirt, and rocks in a pan until the heavier gold settles to the bottom of the pan. Finding gold this way can take a long time. Another way to mine for gold is to use a rocker box, also known as a cradle. Using a wooden box, a person sifts through dirt and sand with a strainer that is at the bottom of the cradle. This is called cradling. The dirt and sediment sifts through but the gold is left behind.

To find gold in a very large area of land, miners used to use hydraulic mining. On hillsides where gold was likely to be found, miners used high-powered water cannons to spray down the hills and wash away the soil. The gravel loosened by this was washed through sieves. There, the heavy gold settled and was left behind while the rest of the dirt washed away. However, hydraulic mining was banned over one hundred years ago because the process hurt the environment.

Answer the items.

1. If you were to try to find gold, would you use a pan or a rocker box? Explain your answer.

   _____

   _____

2. Which method do you think is best for finding the most gold?

   _____

   _____

Skill Sharpeners: Geography • EMC 3743 • © Evan-Moor Corp.

Environment and Society

A miner using a hydraulic jet of water to mine for gold in California—from *Century Magazine,* January 1883

A gold prospector pouring water through his rocker box in Pinos Altos, New Mexico

Environment and Society

Australian Gold

Concept:
The location of resources affects patterns of settlement and trade.

Environment and Society

One famous area for finding gold is the country of Australia. In 1851, the first grain of gold was discovered near the city of Bathurst. Soon, the area was renamed Ophir. Ophir is a city mentioned in the Bible that was known for its wealth. Within four months, over 1,000 prospectors came there to try to strike it rich. Gold fever then spread across Australia, and miners rushed to the diggings.

Gold was also found in many other areas in Australia. In the state of New South Wales, over 26 metric tons (57,320 pounds) of gold was found in 1852 alone. The neighboring state of Victoria found even more gold than that. Soon, hundreds of thousands of immigrants arrived in the country to mine the goldfields. During the 1850s, the state of Victoria alone produced more than one third of the gold mined elsewhere in the world. Gold was found in even more parts of the country.

Businesses boomed in towns wherever the miners were. Many hotels, restaurants, and telegraphs were built. People made a lot of money because of the miners. Different ways to ship gold from Australia to faraway places such as London were also developed.

Answer the item.

Why was a part of Australia named Ophir?

_____

_____

_____

**Seven miners and a small gold mine
head frame without shelter, circa 1850**

**Prospectors in Australia rejoice
at finding gold, circa 1850**

Environment and Society

Skill:
Use visual
discrimination

The Rush for Gold

Find these Gold Rush words in the word search.
Hint: Some are backwards.

| australia | ophir | victoria | panning |
| cradling | hydraulic | miners | gold |

l	e	a	t	f	g	p	u	c	k	v	j	u	o	l
r	a	u	i	n	a	i	i	q	s	i	r	y	s	w
i	x	h	c	n	i	l	g	o	q	c	s	j	n	t
l	y	q	n	c	u	d	n	r	c	t	g	b	o	d
k	a	i	j	a	r	s	u	w	j	o	l	p	n	f
r	n	x	r	u	d	a	x	g	s	r	o	l	x	m
g	n	d	e	a	h	w	d	d	y	i	j	t	l	r
a	y	s	r	e	n	i	m	l	i	a	j	g	o	c
h	w	f	j	w	h	b	c	o	i	i	c	k	s	n
o	z	j	v	h	r	e	u	g	s	n	h	j	y	g
b	h	t	k	e	q	i	f	y	v	w	g	u	l	a
q	w	l	m	v	r	e	h	j	l	h	a	u	k	b
x	v	s	d	d	v	s	h	p	i	r	a	y	x	r
a	u	s	t	r	a	l	i	a	o	e	o	f	j	t
i	s	t	y	s	r	w	d	v	q	i	r	n	u	k

Skill Sharpeners: Geography • EMC 3743 • © Evan-Moor Corp.

Environment and Society

Panning for Gold

Invite your family and friends to pan for "gold"!

What You Need

- shallow, round metal pan
- small rocks, pebbles, and marbles
- water
- gold spray paint
- newspaper
- sand or dirt area

What You Do

1. Find a handful of small pebbles and rocks. You can also use small marbles.

2. Spread out the rocks or marbles on newspaper and spray paint them gold. Allow them to dry completely. Then count the number of gold pieces you have.

3. Bury the gold in dirt. Be sure to remember where you buried all the pieces.

4. Invite a friend or family member to use the pan to scoop out a bunch of dirt. Mix in some water. Now have the person swirl the pan slowly and tilt it so that the dirt falls out while the gold settles. Eventually, the gold pieces will be all that is left in the pan.

5. Keep panning until all of the gold is found!

Environment and Society

Skill:
Write narrative text about real-world situations

Gold Is Special!

Pretend you found a huge gold nugget. What would you do with it? Would you turn it in for money? Would you have it made into a piece of jewelry? Write to tell about it.

_____

_____

_____

_____

_____

_____

_____

_____

_____

_____

_____

_____

_____

_____

Environment and Society

Concept:

Historical events are influenced by geographic context.

Ishi = Man

On August 29, 1911, a man called Ishi walked out of the woods and into the town of Oroville, California. Ishi was not an ordinary man. He was a Native American who had lived alone in the woods for a long time. Experts called Ishi the last wild Native American. I thought a lot about Ishi and his people. I imagined I was talking to him…

"Why were you alone when you came into Oroville?" I asked.

Many of my tribe and family were killed. Others died of diseases. I had been alone near my homeland for a long time when I could no longer find enough food. That is when I came into a town. I was nearly starving.

"How did you get the name Ishi?" I wondered aloud.

I had no name, as there was no one in my tribe left to name me. But Ishi means "man." That was the name the people from the town gave me.

"After you were taken to the museum to live, what did you do?"

I showed people how the members of my tribe lived, got food, and built shelters. I even took some of them back to where I lived in the woods. That was very special, showing people how to live off the natural world. I hope because of that, people got to know my way of life better and could appreciate what we did.

Learning about Ishi made me want to know more about people who existed in the wilderness and lived off the land.

Saxton T. Pope, 1914

The Uses of Geography

Concept:
Historical events are influenced by geographic context.

The Uses of Geography

Lewis and Clark

Define It!

Louisiana Purchase: a land deal between the United States and France, in which the U.S. acquired the land west of the Mississippi River

route: places to travel along from one place to another

geography: the natural features of a place, such as rivers and mountains

In 1803, the United States purchased a large piece of land from the French. This land stretched approximately 828,000 square miles (2,144,510 square kilometers) from the Mississippi River all the way to the Rocky Mountains. The land deal was called the Louisiana Purchase. President Jefferson arranged for a group of about 50 men to explore this large area of land and beyond. The group of army volunteers was led by Meriwether Lewis and William Clark. It has since been called the Lewis and Clark Expedition.

Along the way, the group encountered many Native Americans. They befriended one named Sacagawea. She came along with the group to help interpret native languages and calm native groups that may be unfriendly to the explorers.

The Lewis and Clark Expedition had several goals. One was to explore and map the new territory. Another was to find an easy-to-follow, safe route across the country. They also wanted to help establish an American presence in the land before other countries tried to claim it, or take ownership of it. Finally, the Lewis and Clark Expedition studied the plants, animals, and geography of the area.

The journey from St. Louis, Missouri, to the Pacific Ocean and back took two years, four months, and ten days and lasted from May 1804 to September 1806. When the group finally reached the ocean (where Fort Clatsop, Oregon, is now), Lewis called out, "Ocean in view!"

Answer the item.

What would you have yelled when you saw the ocean?

_____

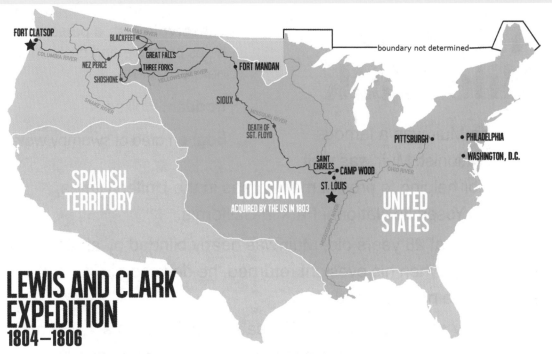

FORT CLATSOP
MARIAS RIVER
BLACKFEET
GREAT FALLS
NEZ PERCE
THREE FORKS
SHOSHONE
COLUMBIA RIVER
YELLOWSTONE RIVER
SNAKE RIVER
FORT MANDAN
SIOUX
MISSOURI RIVER
DEATH OF SGT. FLOYD
SAINT CHARLES
CAMP WOOD
ST. LOUIS
MISSISSIPPI RIVER

boundary not determined

PITTSBURGH • PHILADELPHIA
• WASHINGTON, D.C.
OHIO RIVER

SPANISH TERRITORY

LOUISIANA
ACQUIRED BY THE US IN 1803

UNITED STATES

LEWIS AND CLARK EXPEDITION
1804–1806

William Clark

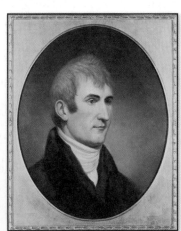

Meriwether Lewis

Sacagawea leading Lewis and Clark through the Louisiana Territory

The Uses of Geography

A 1,000-Mile Walk

Define It!

conservationist: a person who helps preserve and protect the natural world

trodden: walked on

bog: an area of swampy water

John Muir was a famous conservationist. Muir was well known for helping to protect many areas in the United States, including Yosemite National Park in California.

In 1867 at 28 years old, Muir was nearly blinded by an accident in a factory. When his eyesight returned, he devoted his life to studying the natural world.

Shortly after the accident, 29-year-old Muir began a 1,000-mile walk. He journeyed from Indiana to Florida, taking him nearly two years. In Muir's words, he had no certain route or path to take. But he wanted to go on the "wildest, leafiest, and least trodden way I could find." Muir made the journey alone as much as possible.

There were many days Muir went with little food. He also slept nights without blankets. But Muir said he wandered mile after mile as free as the wind. The walk took him through forests, along streams, and next to bogs. The whole time, Muir basked in the beauty of the land. And that journey helped shape the rest of his life.

Answer the item.

Describe what you think Muir's walk was like.

_____

_____

_____

_____

The Uses of Geography

**John Muir at Yosemite
in California**

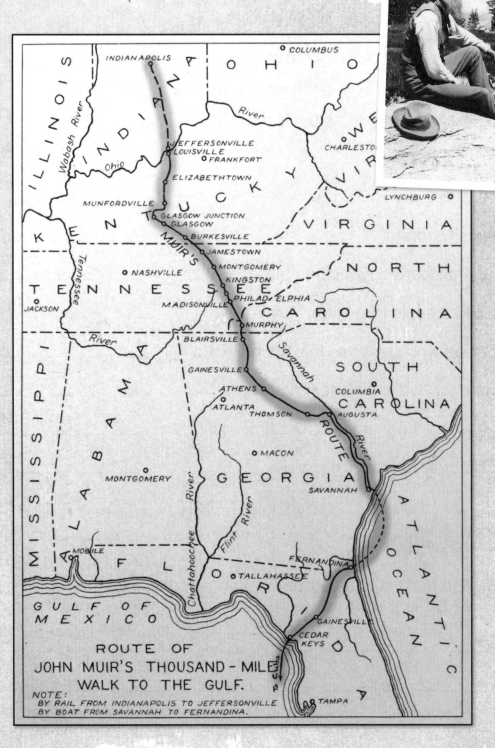

**Map showing John Muir's
1,000-mile journey**

The Uses of Geography

Skill:
Apply geography concepts

Expeditions

Read the description and write the word or words it describes.

trodden	conservationist	bog
route	Louisiana Purchase	Muir
geography	Lewis and Clark	

1. he completed a 1,000-mile walk _____

2. a marshy pond _____

3. land Americans bought from the French _____

4. the path people take when they travel _____

5. a person who preserves the natural world _____

6. a word for "walked along a path" _____

7. men who led a journey across America _____

8. the natural features of a place _____

Think About It

If you had to make a long journey, would you rather go alone or in a group? Explain your answer.

_____

_____

_____

_____

The Uses of Geography

Skill Sharpeners: Geography • EMC 3743 • © Evan-Moor Corp.

Skill:
Apply geography concepts in real-world situations

Expedition Supplies

Put together a supply kit for Ishi or John Muir.

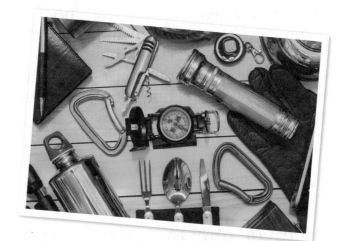

What You Need

- various supplies for food, shelter, and first aid
- container or pack to put everything in

What You Do

1. Decide if you are going to make an emergency kit for Ishi or for John Muir.

2. In the area at right, list all the supplies that you could find in your house that would have helped Ishi or John Muir survive in the wilderness.

3. Place the supplies in the container or pack.

4. Ask someone to pretend that he or she is Ishi or John Muir. Explain to that person what each of the items you gathered is for.

The Uses of Geography

Expedition Journal

There have been many people who have taken long journeys or spent time in the wilderness alone. Pretend that you are one of those people. Write a journal entry that tells where you are, how long you have been there, and what you have seen.

_____

_____

_____

_____

_____

_____

_____

_____

_____

_____

_____

_____

Answer Key

Page 6

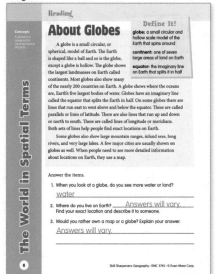

About Globes

Reading

globe: a small circular and hollow scale model of Earth that spins around

continent: one of seven large areas of land on Earth

equator: the imaginary line on Earth that splits it in half

A globe is a small circular, or spherical, model of Earth. The Earth is shaped like a ball and so is the globe, except a globe is hollow. The globe shows the largest landmasses on Earth called continents. Most globes also show many of the nearly 200 countries on Earth. A globe shows where the oceans are, Earth's five largest bodies of water. Globes have an imaginary line called the equator that splits the Earth in half. On some globes there are lines that run east to west above and below the equator. These are called parallels or lines of latitude. There are also lines that run up and down or north to south. These are called lines of longitude or meridians. Both sets of lines help people find exact locations on Earth.

Some globes also show large mountain ranges, inland seas, long rivers, and very large lakes. A few major cities are usually shown on globes as well. When people need to see more detailed information about locations on Earth, they use a map.

Answer the items.

1. When you look at a globe, do you see more water or land?
   water

2. Where do you live on Earth? **Answers will vary.**
   Find your exact location and describe it to someone.

3. Would you rather own a map or a globe? Explain your answer.
   Answers will vary.

Page 8

Earth from Space

Reading

atmosphere: the air and other gases that surround Earth

storm: a weather event caused by low pressure that brings clouds and rain and strong winds

poles: the two areas at the very top and bottom of Earth

Earth is visible from space. Space is anywhere beyond Earth's atmosphere. Our atmosphere is made up of the air and other gases that surround Earth. When looking at our planet from space, several things become clear. First, the Earth is mostly water. About 71% of the Earth's surface is water. Second, there is also water in the Earth's atmosphere. You can see this water in the swirling white areas of clouds above the planet. Clouds are actually billions of water droplets suspended, or hanging, in the air. An occurrence of bad weather in which there is a lot of rain, snow, or strong winds is a storm. Storms are always in motion because the Earth is constantly spinning. If you take a picture of the Earth today, it will look different tomorrow. The clouds and storms will change in shape and size and be in a new location.

It is clear from space that the Earth is round. It has two poles—the one at its northernmost point is called the North Pole. The one at its southernmost point is called the South Pole.

Answer the items.

1. Describe Earth's atmosphere.
   Earth's atmosphere is made up of air and other gases.

2. If you took a picture of Earth from space on two different days, how might the pictures look different?
   The storms and clouds will have moved or changed in size.

Page 10

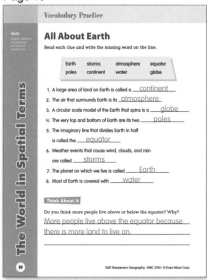

All About Earth

Vocabulary Practice

Read each clue and write the missing word on the line.

| Earth | storms | atmosphere | equator |
| poles | continent | water | globe |

1. A large area of land on Earth is called a **continent**
2. The air that surrounds Earth is its **atmosphere**
3. A circular scale model of the Earth that spins is a **globe**
4. The very top and bottom of Earth are its two **poles**
5. The imaginary line that divides Earth in half is called the **equator**
6. Weather events that cause wind, clouds, and rain are called **storms**
7. The planet on which we live is called **Earth**
8. Most of Earth is covered with **water**

Think About It

Do you think more people live above or below the equator? Why?
More people live above the equator because there is more land to live on.

Page 12

My Finger Landed…

Application

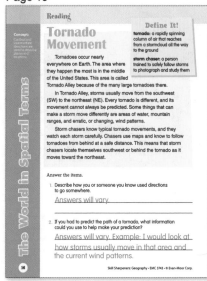

Pretend you are a student in Mrs. Takagawa's class. It is your turn to spin the globe. You put your hand on the globe and spin it. After 2 seconds, you put your finger on it and it skids it to a stop. Write about the location your finger lands on.

- Where is it on Earth?
- Is it on land or in the ocean?
- Is it near the equator?

Writing will vary.

Page 14

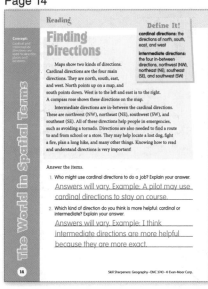

Finding Directions

Reading

cardinal directions: the directions of north, south, east, and west

intermediate directions: the four in-between directions, northwest (NW), northeast (NE), southeast (SE), and southwest (SW)

Maps show two kinds of directions. Cardinal directions are the four main directions. They are north, south, east, and west. North points up on a map, and south points down. West is to the left and east is to the right. A compass rose shows these directions on the map.

Intermediate directions are in-between the cardinal directions. These are northwest (NW), northeast (NE), southwest (SW), and southeast (SE). All of these directions help people in emergencies, such as avoiding a tornado. Directions are also needed to find a route to and from school or a store. They may help locate a lost dog, fight a fire, plan a long hike, and many other things. Knowing how to read and understand directions is very important!

Answer the items.

1. Who might use cardinal directions to do a job? Explain your answer.
   Answers will vary. Example: A pilot may use cardinal directions to stay on course.

2. Which kind of direction do you think is more helpful: cardinal or intermediate? Explain your answer.
   Answers will vary. Example: I think intermediate directions are more helpful because they are more exact.

Page 16

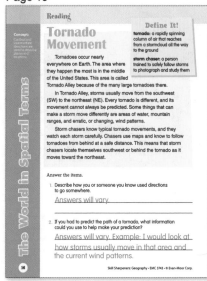

Tornado Movement

Reading

tornado: a rapidly spinning column of air that reaches from a stormcloud all the way to the ground

storm chaser: a person trained to safely follow storms to photograph and study them

Tornadoes occur nearly everywhere on Earth. The area where they happen the most is in the middle of the United States. This area is called Tornado Alley because of the many large tornadoes there.

In Tornado Alley, storms usually move from the southwest (SW) to the northeast (NE). Every tornado is different, and its movement cannot always be predicted. Some things that can make a storm move differently are areas of water, mountain ranges, and erratic, or changing, wind patterns.

Storm chasers know typical tornado movements, and they watch each storm carefully. Chasers use maps and know to follow tornadoes from behind at a safe distance. This means that storm chasers locate themselves southwest or behind the tornado as it moves toward the northeast.

Answer the items.

1. Describe how you or someone you know used directions to go somewhere.
   Answers will vary.

2. If you had to predict the path of a tornado, what information could you use to help make your prediction?
   Answers will vary. Example: I would look at how storms usually move in that area and the current wind patterns.

Page 18

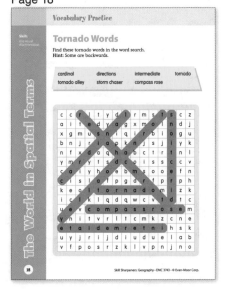

Tornado Words

Vocabulary Practice

Find these tornado words in the word search.
Hint: Some are backwards.

| cardinal | directions | intermediate | tornado |
| tornado alley | storm chaser | compass rose | |

Page 20

You Are in Charge!

Application

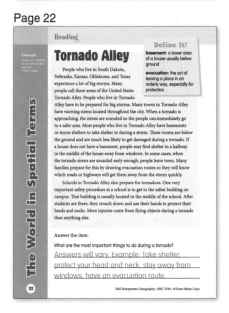

Pretend you are traveling with a group of storm chasers and you are the expert. Your job is to make sure everyone is safe.

- What should you do?
- What would you say to make everyone feel safe?
- What can you tell the others about tornadoes?

Writing will vary.

Page 22

Tornado Alley

Reading

basement: a lower area of a house usually below ground

evacuation: the act of leaving a place in an orderly way, especially for protection

People who live in South Dakota, Nebraska, Kansas, Oklahoma, and Texas experience a lot of big storms. Many people call these areas of the United States Tornado Alley. People who live in Tornado Alley have to be prepared for big storms. Many towns in Tornado Alley have warning sirens located throughout the city. When a tornado is approaching, the sirens are sounded so the people can immediately go to a safer area. Most people who live in Tornado Alley have basements or storm shelters to take shelter in during a storm. These rooms are below the ground and are much less likely to get damaged during a tornado. If a house does not have a basement, people may find shelter in a hallway in the middle of the house away from windows. In some cases, when the tornado sirens are sounded early enough, people leave town. Many families prepare for this by drawing evacuation routes so they will know which roads or highways will get them away from the storm quickly.

Schools in Tornado Alley also prepare for tornadoes. One very important safety procedure at a school is to get to the safest building on campus. That building is usually located in the middle of the school. After students are there, they crouch down and use their hands to protect their heads and necks. More injuries come from flying objects during a tornado than anything else.

Answer the item.

What are the most important things to do during a tornado?
Answers will vary. Example: Take shelter, protect your head and neck, stay away from windows, have an evacuation route.

Page 24

Reading

Earthquake and Fire!

Define It!

earthquake drill: the procedure used to keep people safe during an earthquake

fire drill: the procedure used to keep people safe during a fire

Many schools have earthquake and fire drills. During an earthquake drill, students are told to "drop, cover, and hold." This means that students need to drop to their knees, cover their heads and necks, and hold still. They are also told to get under a sturdy desk or table to protect themselves from falling objects like books or art supplies. Heavier items such as shelving units are usually bolted to the walls so that they will not fall over during an earthquake. If students cannot get under a desk, they may be told to stand in a doorway because it provides some safety for them. After the earthquake is over, all students evacuate, or leave, the building in case it is no longer safe.

When schools have fire drills, each class has an evacuation route or a plan to follow. The students and teachers and anyone else who works at the school practice what to do if there is a fire. The drill begins when the fire alarm rings. Students line up and quietly follow their teacher to the safe place that is shown on the fire escape route map. Schools' leaders make the fire escape route maps by planning the best way for everyone at the school to get out of the buildings safely. The routes are reviewed by school leaders and sometimes even the fire department to make sure they are the best ones possible for a real emergency.

Answer the item.

What might the fire department look for during a fire drill to make sure it was safe?

Answers will vary. Example: The fire department might make sure the students are taking the shortest path to get away from the school.

The World in Spatial Terms

24 Skill Sharpeners: Geography • EMC 3743 • © Evan-Moor Corp.

Page 26

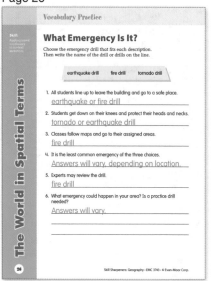

Vocabulary Practice

What Emergency Is It?

Choose the emergency drill that fits each description. Then write the name of the drill or drills on the line.

earthquake drill fire drill tornado drill

1. All students line up to leave the building and go to a safe place. earthquake or fire drill
2. Students get down on their knees and protect their heads and necks. tornado or earthquake drill
3. Classes follow maps and go to their assigned areas. fire drill
4. It is the least common emergency of the three choices. Answers will vary, depending on location.
5. Experts may review the drill. fire drill
6. What emergency could happen in your area? Is a practice drill needed? Answers will vary.

The World in Spatial Terms

26 Skill Sharpeners: Geography • EMC 3743 • © Evan-Moor Corp.

Page 28

Application

Be Prepared!

Think about the things you and your family may need to be prepared for an emergency. Make a shopping list of things for your family to buy so you can create an emergency kit.

Shopping List for Our Emergency Kit

- bottled water
- canned foods
- can opener
- nuts
- dried fruit
- flashlight
- batteries
- blankets

The World in Spatial Terms

28 Skill Sharpeners: Geography • EMC 3743 • © Evan-Moor Corp.

Page 30

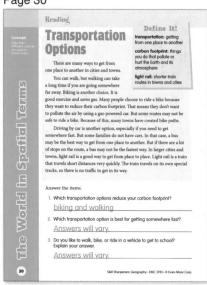

Reading

Transportation Options

Define It!

transportation: getting from one place to another

carbon footprint: things you do that pollute or hurt the Earth and its atmosphere

light rail: shorter train routes in towns and cities

There are many ways to get from one place to another in cities and towns.

You can walk, but walking can take a long time if you are going somewhere far away. Biking is another choice. It is good exercise and saves gas. Many people choose to ride a bike because they want to reduce their carbon footprint. That means they don't want to pollute the air by using a gas-powered car. But some routes may not be safe to ride a bike. Because of this, many towns have created bike paths.

Driving by car is another option, especially if you need to get somewhere fast. But some families do not have cars. In that case, a bus may be the best way to get from one place to another. But if there are a lot of stops on the route, a bus may not be the fastest way. In larger cities and towns, light rail is a good way to get from place to place. Light rail is a train that travels short distances very quickly. The train travels on its own special tracks, so there is no traffic to get in its way.

Answer the items.

1. Which transportation options reduce your carbon footprint? biking and walking
2. Which transportation option is best for getting somewhere fast? Answers will vary.
3. Do you like to walk, bike, or ride in a vehicle to get to school? Explain your answer. Answers will vary.

The World in Spatial Terms

30 Skill Sharpeners: Geography • EMC 3743 • © Evan-Moor Corp.

Page 32

Reading

Transportation Maps

Define It!

destination: a place a person is traveling to

ground transportation: cars, buses, and trains used to travel from one location to another

symbol: a picture that stands for something

People who are traveling long distances have many options. Some people choose to drive a vehicle. They must think about the route they will take and how much time it will take to get to their final destination. People who are traveling long distances may choose to fly. Most countries have international airports in large cities. People who travel by air fly with hundreds of other passengers and may have to take more than one flight to get to their final destination. Some people prefer to travel by train. Train stations are usually located in large cities. Traveling by boat is another option. Boats take passengers across bays and oceans, and through canals, or man-made waterways.

Sometimes, people have to take more than one type of transportation to get to their final destination. For example, a person who wants to go to Monterey, California, might fly to San Francisco airport and then take ground transportation, such as a shuttle or a rental car, and drive two hours south to Monterey. Many cities have bus and subway systems or light rails that take people to locations in the city or nearby cities. Transportation options are shown on maps with symbols that show the travel choices available in each area.

Answer the items.

1. When is ground transportation used? after long travel by plane, train, or boat
2. What is the best way to travel long distances? Answers will vary.

The World in Spatial Terms

32 Skill Sharpeners: Geography • EMC 3743 • © Evan-Moor Corp.

Page 34

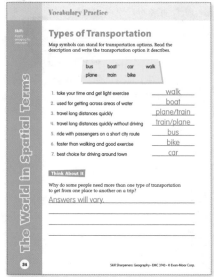

Vocabulary Practice

Types of Transportation

Map symbols can stand for transportation options. Read the description and write the transportation option it describes.

bus boat car walk plane train bike

1. take your time and get light exercise walk
2. used for getting across areas of water boat
3. travel long distances quickly plane/train
4. travel long distances quickly without driving train/plane
5. ride with passengers on a short city route bus
6. faster than walking and good exercise bike
7. best choice for driving around town car

Think About It

Why do some people need more than one type of transportation to get from one place to another on a trip?

Answers will vary.

The World in Spatial Terms

34 Skill Sharpeners: Geography • EMC 3743 • © Evan-Moor Corp.

Page 36

Application

Now You Are Getting Somewhere!

Write about how to get to a place in your town. Examples: a school, a store, a park, a museum, or a friend's house. The starting point is your house.

Plan how you will get to this location.
- What transportation method will you use?
- Will you need more than one form of transportation?
- How long will it take you to get there?

Writing will vary.

The World in Spatial Terms

36 Skill Sharpeners: Geography • EMC 3743 • © Evan-Moor Corp.

Page 38

Reading

Mountains All Over Earth

Define It!

mountain range: a group of connected mountains

glacier: a large body of ice that moves slowly

Mt. Everest is the tallest mountain in the world. It is 29,029 feet (8,848 m) high. Mt. Everest is part of the Himalaya Mountains of Asia. This mountain range has the ten highest peaks in the world, including Everest. The Himalayas are in the countries of India, Nepal, Bhutan, Tibet, Pakistan, and Afghanistan. This region is known for frigid weather at high elevations and massive glaciers.

There are other major mountain ranges on Earth. The rugged Alps of Europe stretch into eight countries, including Switzerland, Austria, Germany, and France. The Andes of South America are the longest mountain range in the world. They are in seven countries, including Chile, Ecuador, Argentina, and Peru. The Rocky Mountains of North America stretch from the southwest of the United States to northern British Columbia in Canada. Another very well-known mountain range is the Sierra Nevada in eastern California. Sierra Nevada is Spanish for "snowy range." Just north of the Sierras is the Cascade Range of volcanoes that stretch from northern California to southern British Columbia, Canada.

Answer the items.

1. What do the mountain ranges in the text have in common? Answers will vary. They are in many countries.
2. Would you like to visit the longest mountain range in the world or the highest? Explain your answer. Answers will vary.

Places and Regions

38 Skill Sharpeners: Geography • EMC 3743 • © Evan-Moor Corp.

Page 40

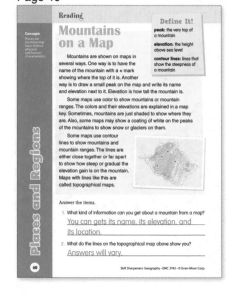

Reading

Mountains on a Map

Define It!

peak: the very top of a mountain

elevation: the height above sea level

contour lines: lines that show the steepness of a mountain

Mountains are shown on maps in several ways. One way is to have the name of the mountain with a + mark showing where the top of it is. Another way is to draw a small peak on the map and write its name and elevation next to it. Elevation is how tall the mountain is.

Some maps use color to show mountains or mountain ranges. The colors and their elevations are explained in a map key. Sometimes, mountains are just shaded to show where they are. Also, some maps may show a coating of white on the peaks of the mountains to show snow or glaciers on them.

Some maps use contour lines to show mountains and mountain ranges. The lines are either close together or far apart to show how steep or gradual the elevation gain is on the mountain. Maps with lines like this are called topographical maps.

Answer the items.

1. What kind of information can you get about a mountain from a map? You can gets its name, its elevation, and its location.
2. What do the lines on the topographical map above show you? Answers will vary.

Places and Regions

40 Skill Sharpeners: Geography • EMC 3743 • © Evan-Moor Corp.

Page 42

Vocabulary Practice

Skill: Apply content vocabulary in context

Mountain Parts

Write the correct word or words to label the picture.

peak   glacier   mountain range
contour lines   volcano   elevation

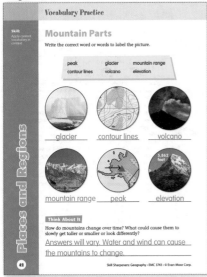

glacier   contour lines   volcano

mountain range   peak   elevation

Think About It

How do mountains change over time? What could cause them to slowly get taller or smaller or look differently?

<u>Answers will vary. Water and wind can cause</u>
<u>the mountains to change.</u>

Skill Sharpeners: Geography • EMC 3743 • © Evan-Moor Corp.

Places and Regions

Page 44

Application

Skill: Write informative text to convey information and experiences clearly

To the Top of the Mountain!

About 800 people try to climb to the top of Mt. Everest each year. Pretend that you are one of the few who reach the summit. Write a journal entry that tells about the climb, how you felt when you reached the top, and what you saw.

<u>Writing will vary.</u>

Skill Sharpeners: Geography • EMC 3743 • © Evan-Moor Corp.

Places and Regions

Page 46

Reading

Concept: Places are locations that have distinct physical and human characteristics

The Mighty Mississippi

A great deal of the land around the Mississippi today is farmland. Farms take water from the river to water their crops. This is called irrigation. Many of those farms use fertilizer and other chemical products to help grow their crops. Some of the waste from that has gone into the Mississippi. Because of this, the water is no longer as clear and clean as it used to be.

The river is used by a lot of boats. Many of them are large boats called barges.

The water of the Mississippi no longer flows freely. All along the river are a series of dams. These were built to generate electricity. Dams also help set up areas on the water for outdoor activities such as boating and fishing. Even though the Mississippi is no longer a freely running wild river, it is still huge! Several large rivers, including the Missouri, Ohio, and Arkansas, feed into it. By the time the Mississippi reaches the Gulf of Mexico, it is the fourth-largest river (measured by the amount of water it pours into the ocean) in the world.

Define It!

irrigation: moving water from one place to another

fertilizer: chemical and natural products given to crops to help their growth

barge: a long boat with a flat bottom used for carrying goods

dam: a man-made structure that blocks river water from flowing

tributaries: rivers that flow into another river, making it grow larger

Answer the items.

1. Do you think farmers should be allowed to grow crops along the Mississippi? Explain your answer.
<u>Answers will vary.</u>

2. What can you learn about the Mississippi River by looking at the photos and the map?
<u>Answers will vary.</u>

Skill Sharpeners: Geography • EMC 3743 • © Evan-Moor Corp.

Places and Regions

Page 48

Reading

Concept: Places are locations that have distinct physical and human characteristics

The Blue Danube

The Danube River in Europe has an even longer history than the Mississippi. Along its route are remains of some of the earliest human settlements. Near it are castles and fortresses built hundreds of years ago. The river was once an important border for countries of the past.

The Danube is the second-longest river in Europe. It travels 1,777 miles (2,860 km) from Germany to the Black Sea. It passes through parts of ten countries, including Germany, Austria, Hungary, and Romania.

Just like the Mississippi, the Danube supplies water for people and farms. There are also hydroelectric dams on the Danube that generate electricity. Another use of the river is to transport goods on boats.

Finally, the Danube is known as a scenic river. Several of the beautiful cities it passes include Ulm in Germany, Vienna in Austria, and Budapest in Hungary. These cities are known as popular tourist areas where people take vacations. Many people take cruises on the Danube, and there are many miles of bike paths along its shores.

Define It!

fortress: a fort used by the military to secure an area

hydroelectric: using moving water to make electricity

tourist: a person who is on vacation in a certain area

Answer the items.

1. If you went on a Danube River cruise, what would you want to see the most?
<u>Answers will vary.</u>

2. In what ways are the Danube and the Mississippi similar?
<u>Answers will vary.</u>

Skill Sharpeners: Geography • EMC 3743 • © Evan-Moor Corp.

Places and Regions

Page 50

Vocabulary Practice

Skill: Apply content vocabulary in context

River Words

Use these words to label the pictures.

barge   dam   canoe
castle   irrigation   farm

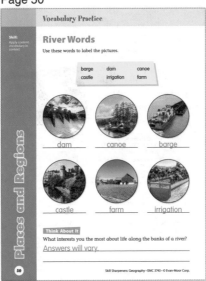

dam   canoe   barge

castle   farm   irrigation

Think About It

What interests you the most about life along the banks of a river?

<u>Answers will vary.</u>

Skill Sharpeners: Geography • EMC 3743 • © Evan-Moor Corp.

Places and Regions

Page 52

Application

Skill: Write informative text to convey information and experiences clearly

Water Near You

What body of water is near your town? Does your community use it for recreation, as a water source, or both? Think about what you know. Then ask your parents to help you find more information about a major river or lake near your town. Write about it and how it is used.

<u>Writing will vary.</u>

Skill Sharpeners: Geography • EMC 3743 • © Evan-Moor Corp.

Places and Regions

Page 54

Reading

Concept: Physical processes shape features of Earth's surface

Yellowstone Is Hot!

The ground beneath Yellowstone National Park is part of a caldera, or a collapsed volcano. The eruption that occurred at Yellowstone just over 600,000 years ago made the crust, or top layer of the Earth, there incredibly thin.

Hot water beneath the ground at Yellowstone rises up toward the Earth's surface. It reaches the surface in amazing ways. The most famous hot-water feature at the park is Old Faithful Geyser. A geyser is where boiling water sprays up out of the ground. Old Faithful Geyser shoots water up to 180 feet (55 m) into the air once every hour or so. There are over 300 geysers at Yellowstone. There are also many steam vents called fumaroles. These are places where steam hisses through a hole in the ground. Yellowstone also has deep, hot pools and large boiling springs. There are also pits of boiling and plopping mud.

There are over 10,000 of these hot-water features at Yellowstone, which is more than any place in the world. Many people come from all over the world to see them.

Define It!

caldera: a collapsed volcano

fumarole: a hole in the ground that lets out steam and other gases

geyser: a place where very hot to boiling water sprays out of the ground

Answer the items.

1. Why is there so much hot water coming out of the ground at Yellowstone?
<u>The hot core of the Earth is not very far</u>
<u>below the ground due to an ancient volcano.</u>

2. How would you make sure visitors stay safe around the hot water?
<u>Answers will vary.</u>

Skill Sharpeners: Geography • EMC 3743 • © Evan-Moor Corp.

Physical Systems

Page 56

Reading

Concept: Physical processes shape features of Earth's surface

Ring of Fire

The Ring of Fire is a horseshoe-shaped area around the Pacific Ocean. Many volcanic eruptions have occurred in the Ring of Fire. Some of the most active countries in the Ring of Fire are Japan, Indonesia, Mexico, Chile, Guatemala, New Zealand, the Philippines, and Ecuador. These places are known for their frequent volcanic activity.

The Ring of Fire was created by tectonic plates, or huge slabs of solid rock, moving like giant rafts on the Earth's surface. These plates sometimes slide next to, collide with, and are forced underneath each other. The Pacific Plate and the surrounding plates do this often, causing earthquakes. When the plates collide, this also creates a huge amount of energy. The energy melts rocks into magma, or hot, molten rock. This magma then rises to the surface as lava and forms volcanoes. There are more than 450 volcanoes along the Ring of Fire.

Define It!

tectonic plates: huge slabs of the Earth's crust that move slowly

earthquake: when Earth's plates collide, it causes the ground to shake

volcano: a mountain with a hole in it that sometimes sends out gases or lava

Answer the items.

1. What is the difference between an earthquake and a volcano?
<u>Earthquakes are when the ground shakes.</u>
<u>Volcanoes have lava that flows out.</u>

2. Which would you be more afraid of: an earthquake or a volcano?
<u>Answers will vary.</u>

3. How close do you live to the Ring of Fire?
<u>Answers will vary.</u>

Skill Sharpeners: Geography • EMC 3743 • © Evan-Moor Corp.

Physical Systems

Page 58

Vocabulary Practice

Skill: Apply content vocabulary in context

Active Earth

Solve the crossword puzzle with words you now know!

caldera   ring of fire   tectonic plate   core
volcano   geyser   earthquake

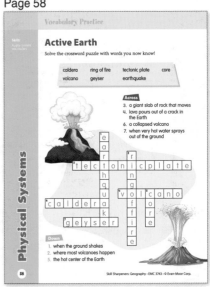

Across

3. a giant slab of rock that moves
4. lava pours out of a crack in the Earth
6. a collapsed volcano
7. when very hot water sprays out of the ground

Down

1. when the ground shakes
2. where most volcanoes happen
5. the hot center of the Earth

Skill Sharpeners: Geography • EMC 3743 • © Evan-Moor Corp.

Physical Systems

Page 60

Skill: ...

Application

A Trip to Yellowstone!

Yellowstone National Park is the world's first national park. It was created in 1872. Over four million people visit Yellowstone every year. Many come to see the hot-water features.

Write to tell what features you would like to see at Yellowstone National Park. Explain what you think it will be like to see the features in person.

Writing will vary.

Physical Systems

Skill Sharpeners: Geography • EMC 3743 • © Evan-Moor Corp.

Page 62

Reading

Deserts All Over the World

Define It!
desert: a hot or cold place with little precipitation
precipitation: rain, hail, sleet, or snow
evaporation: water disappearing into the air

Death Valley is part of the Mojave and Colorado Deserts of North America. Deserts are places on Earth that get very little precipitation. Deserts also have more evaporation than rain or snow. That means what little water they get quickly disappears into the air. There are deserts all over the world, and most of them are hot like Death Valley. But there are cold deserts, too, including the Arctic and Antarctica.

The largest hot desert is the Sahara. It is on the continent of Africa. The Sahara is huge—about the size of China and the United States put together. The Sahara is known for having vast areas of endless sand dunes blowing in the wind.

A large part of Australia is desert. Most of the western part of the country is incredibly dry. There are some scattered small towns and cities in the desert of Australia, which some people call the Outback.

The Atacama Desert of Chile is the driest desert in the world. It is so dry that some parts of it have never seen a drop of rain. In other parts of the Atacama, people have said the rocky soil and lack of plants make it look like Mars.

Answer the items.

1. Do you want to visit a desert? Why or why not?
   Answers will vary.

2. How do you think you would feel while walking in the Sahara Desert?
   Answers will vary.

Physical Systems

Skill Sharpeners: Geography • EMC 3743 • © Evan-Moor Corp.

Page 64

Reading

Biomes All Over the World

Define It!
biome: an area of plants, animals, and insects that live and work together
tundra: a cold, frozen area with tiny plants
taiga: a cold, moist forested area

Deserts are one type of biome on Earth. A biome is where all living things in that area—the plants, animals, and insects—work together as a community.

Another type of biome is a grassland. This is a large area with small plants, shrubs, and grasses. It is too wet to be a desert and too dry for trees. This is also sometimes called a savanna.

Tundra is another biome. This is a mostly cold area with only tiny plants. Most of the year, tundra is covered in snow and ice. There are no trees because the weather is far too cold. Tundra occurs toward the North Pole or on the peaks of high, cold mountains.

Forests are another type of biome. A tropical rainforest has an incredible amount of living things in it. Tropical rainforests are also hot, humid, and rainy. Temperate rainforests have a warm season and a cool one. They also get a lot of rain and are thick with trees. Finally, there is the taiga forest. This area is moist and cold most of the year. Taiga plants, such as pine and fir trees, are typically evergreen, so their leaves don't change color.

Answer the items.

1. In which biome do you live?
   Answers will vary.

2. Which biome would you want to go visit on vacation? Tell why.
   Answers will vary.

Physical Systems

Skill Sharpeners: Geography • EMC 3743 • © Evan-Moor Corp.

Page 66

Vocabulary Practice

The World's Biomes

Match the word or words to its description.

taiga   tropical rainforest   savanna   precipitation
tundra   temperate rainforest   desert

1. a forested area that is cold and moist — taiga
2. an area of mostly grasses and some shrubs — savanna
3. warm, rainy, and lots of plants and animals — tropical rainforest
4. rainy with seasons, lots of trees — temperate rainforest
5. rain, hail, sleet, or snow — precipitation
6. a place that gets little rain — desert
7. very cold, so few plants can grow — tundra

Think About It

Draw your favorite biome.

Drawings will vary.

Physical Systems

Skill Sharpeners: Geography • EMC 3743 • © Evan-Moor Corp.

Page 67

Hands-on Activity

Desert at Your House?

In this activity, you will explore outside around your house to find out what locations are warmer than others.

What You Need
• thermometers   • paper   • pencil

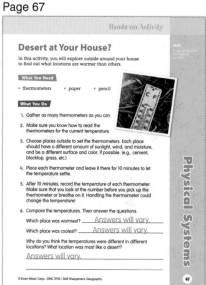

What You Do

1. Gather as many thermometers as you can.
2. Make sure you know how to read the thermometers for the current temperature.
3. Choose places outside to set the thermometers. Each place should have a different amount of sunlight, wind, and moisture, and be a different surface and color, if possible. (e.g., cement, blacktop, grass, etc.)
4. Place each thermometer and leave it there for 10 minutes to let the temperature settle.
5. After 10 minutes, record the temperature of each thermometer. Make sure that you look at the number before you pick up the thermometer or breathe on it. Handling the thermometer could change the temperature!
6. Compare the temperatures. Then answer the questions.
   Which place was warmest? Answers will vary.
   Which place was coolest? Answers will vary.

   Why do you think the temperatures were different in different locations? What location was most like a desert?
   Answers will vary.

Physical Systems

© Evan-Moor Corp. • EMC 3743 • Skill Sharpeners: Geography

Page 68

Application

Going to the Desert

Deserts are often hot and always dry. However, many people live in deserts. People also vacation in them to see their amazing scenery, plants, and animals.

Pretend you are going away to the desert. Write what you'd like to see and what you need to bring to make your journey safe and comfortable.

Writing will vary.

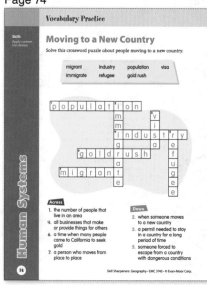

Physical Systems

Skill Sharpeners: Geography • EMC 3743 • © Evan-Moor Corp.

Page 70

Reading

Going to California

Define It!
Gold Rush: the period of time when many people came to California hoping to find gold
population: the number of people living in an area
industry: all the businesses that make or do a particular type of thing

People have been moving to California for a long time! It started with the Gold Rush in the mid-1800s. Miners went there to try and strike it rich in the goldfields. Other people went to California to start businesses or provide services to the miners.

In the 1900s, California's population continued to grow. The fertile San Joaquin Valley of California became, and still is, one of the most important farming regions in the world. Industry, or the making of goods and services, is also well known in California. One of those industries is moviemaking. In the 1920s and '30s, Hollywood in Southern California became the film center of the world. Many movies were made there. Some of the movies showed the California lifestyle, which included sunny beaches, warm mountain hikes, and happy people at Disneyland. Those movies inspired even more people to move to California.

The computer industry's boom started in the 1980s and '90s in an area south of San Francisco called Silicon Valley. It was named after the silicon chips used in computers. Today, California has a population of over 39 million people, making it the most populated state in the United States.

Answer the items.

1. What question do you have about the state of California?
   Answers will vary.

2. Would you want to live in California? Why or why not?
   Answers will vary.

Human Systems

Skill Sharpeners: Geography • EMC 3743 • © Evan-Moor Corp.

Page 72

Reading

A New Place to Call Home

Define It!
migrant: a person who moves from one place to another
immigrant: a person who moves to another country
refugee: a person forced to move from his or her homeland because of dangerous conditions

The world has over 7 billion people living in it. Over 200 million of these people are called migrants. They have moved, or immigrated, to another country. Some people leave their homeland to find better jobs or a better education. Some people move to find better living conditions. Some people have to leave their home because of wars or lack of food. Many countries help these refugees.

The countries that have the most people migrating to them are the United States, Russia, Germany, Saudi Arabia, Canada, and the United Kingdom. But sometimes countries decide not to allow many people to enter their country.

Countries also have passport and visa requirements to get in. A passport is needed for a short trip such as a vacation. A visa is needed if a person has a job and needs to stay in the country for many years. Applying for a visa can include medical exams, vaccination forms, education, and other things to make sure an immigrating person is healthy and able to afford living in the country.

Answer the items.

1. Has anyone in your family moved from one country to another? What was the reason?
   Answers will vary.

2. Do you have a passport? If so, which countries have you visited?
   Answers will vary.

Human Systems

Skill Sharpeners: Geography • EMC 3743 • © Evan-Moor Corp.

Page 74

Vocabulary Practice

Moving to a New Country

Solve this crossword puzzle about people moving to a new country.

migrant   industry   population   visa
immigrate   refugee   gold rush

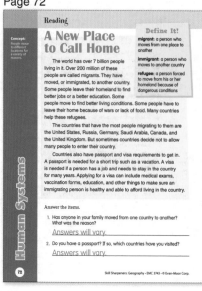

p o p u l a t i o n
i n d u s t r y
g o l d r u s h
m i g r a n t

Across
1. the number of people that live in an area
4. all businesses that make or provide things for others
6. a time when many people come to California to seek gold
7. a person who moves from place to place

Down
2. when someone moves to a new country
3. a permit needed to stay in a country for a long period of time
5. someone forced to escape from a country with dangerous conditions

Human Systems

Skill Sharpeners: Geography • EMC 3743 • © Evan-Moor Corp.

Page 76

Time to Move!

Pretend you have to immigrate to another country. How would you feel about moving? What would you bring with you? What would you have to leave behind?

Write about the country you are moving to and what you think life will be like.

Writing will vary.

Human Systems

Page 78

Reading

Four Languages in One Country!

Define It!
dialect: a special, local version of an original language

proximity: how close one is to something, such as the proximity to another country

Switzerland is a small country right in the middle of Europe. Over 8 million people live there. Switzerland is surrounded by much larger and more populated countries on all sides. There is Germany to the north, Italy to the south, Austria to the east, and France to the west. Because of its location and history, there are four official languages in the country of Switzerland.

The most common language in Switzerland is Swiss German. The second most common is Swiss French, and the third is Swiss Italian. A small number of people in Switzerland still speak an ancient language called Romansch. Each of the three main languages is a special dialect. That means it is different from the traditional native language spoken in the neighboring country. The language is its own Swiss version of the original language. Also, most people in Switzerland speak and understand some English. The dominant, or most spoken, language of each region in Switzerland depends on its proximity, or location, to the country surrounding it. Most children going to school in Switzerland speak and learn several languages at the same time!

Answer the items.

1. If you lived in Switzerland, what languages would you like to speak?
   Answers will vary.

2. Do you think it is better to learn one language at a time or more than one?
   Answers will vary.

Page 80

Reading

Languages Around the World

Define It!
universal language: a language that is spoken and understood in more places than any other

There are about 6,500 languages spoken throughout the world. The most common languages are Chinese, English, Spanish, Arabic, Hindi, Russian, Portuguese, and French.

English is spoken in more countries than any other language. Many schools in non-English-speaking countries teach English. Because of this, many people call English a universal language.

However, the language that is spoken by the most people is Chinese. The main reason for this is that China is the most populated country on Earth. There are more than 1 billion, 387 million people living in China. Chinese is also spoken in other Asian countries, including Hong Kong, Singapore, Macau, and Taiwan.

Spanish is the third most common language in the world. It is spoken in Spain and Mexico. Spanish is also spoken in many countries of Central and South America, including Costa Rica, Guatemala, Honduras, Chile, and Peru.

Answer the items.

1. What language besides English might be called a universal language?
   Answers will vary.

2. Which of the most common languages would you like to learn? Why?
   Answers will vary.

Page 82

Vocabulary Practice

Many Languages

Find these language-related words in the word search.
Hint: Some are backwards.

dialect proximity switzerland chinese
english spanish native universal

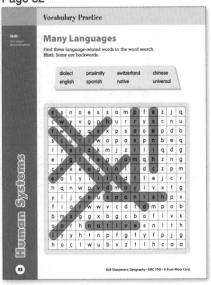

Page 84

Application

Juggling Languages

Write a story about a boy or girl who moves to a new school and does not speak the same language as everyone else. Tell about how the kids at school treat him or her.

Writing will vary.

Page 86

Reading

Green Table

Define It!
Mesa Verde: "green table" in Spanish

preserve: to keep something from being harmed or damaged

drought: a period of time with little or no rain

Mesa Verde National Park is in southwest Colorado in the United States. It was established on June 29, 1906. Much of the park sits high up on flat mountains that turn green in the summer due to thunderstorms. The park is mostly known for the ancient homes, or archaeological sites, of the Ancestral Puebloans. An archaeological site is a location with historical homes, artifacts, or ruins. The homes at Mesa Verde are some of the best preserved in the entire world.

At Mesa Verde there are about 5,000 of these sites, including 600 cliff dwellings, which are the homes the people lived in from AD 1200 to AD 1300. Rangers offer guided tours of many of the ruins all summer long.

For a long time it was a mystery why the people who once lived there left. Experts now believe that a drought forced them to move elsewhere. The Puebloan people could not grow their crops in drought conditions, so they probably left and searched for a new place that had more rainfall.

Answer the items.

1. Why is Mesa Verde called a "green table"?
   The mountains turn green in the summer.

2. Why do you think many of the tours at Mesa Verde are guided by rangers?
   Answers will vary.

3. If you could ask the Puebloans a question, what would you ask them?
   Questions will vary.

Page 88

Reading

Inca Royalty

Define It!
sanctuary: a special place for religious leaders and others

abandoned: to be left behind and forgotten about

artifact: an ancient object made by humans

High up in the Andes Mountains of Peru lies the ancient city of Machu Picchu. Machu Picchu is at nearly 8,000 feet (2,438 m) elevation on a mountain plateau. A plateau is a flat area near the top of a mountain.

Built in the 1400s, Machu Picchu was once a sanctuary, or special religious place, for Inca leaders. The city had over 150 buildings, some of which were homes, bath houses, and temples. These buildings were originally constructed with dry stone walls. In the 1500s, about 100 years after it was built, the Incas were scared away by the conquering Spanish civilization. The Incas left and the city was abandoned.

Machu Picchu was unknown to the world until 1911. In 1911, an American archaeologist stumbled upon the ruins of the lost city. An archaeologist is a person who studies ancient civilizations and their artifacts. By the 1900s, much of the city had been overgrown by the thick, jungle-like plants. And many of the buildings were in disrepair, or broken down. Now Machu Picchu is being reconstructed, or built just like it used to be. Over a million people from all over visit it yearly to see one of the world's most famous man-made wonders.

Answer the items.

1. Why do you think Machu Picchu was built high in the mountains?
   Answers will vary.

2. Why do you think nobody knew about Machu Picchu for about 350 years?
   Answers will vary.

Page 90

Vocabulary Practice

Ancient Sites

Write the word next to its definition.

drought archaeologist abandoned sanctuary
Mesa Verde ruins artifact preserve

1. "green table" in Spanish — Mesa Verde
2. a person who studies the past and its artifacts — archaeologist
3. an item created by people long ago — artifact
4. a special religious place — sanctuary
5. the ancient remains of something — ruins
6. a period of very dry weather — drought
7. to be left behind and forgotten about — abandoned
8. to keep something from being damaged — preserve

Think About It

What might have happened if Machu Picchu and its artifacts had not been discovered?
Answers will vary.

Page 92

Application

Clues to the Past

Artifacts and ruins are clues to the past. How could studying these help tell us what a place was like when it was full of people? Pretend that you are an archaeologist and you have dug up some artifacts. Write about what you found and who you think the items belonged to.

Writing will vary.

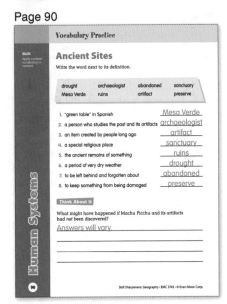

Page 94

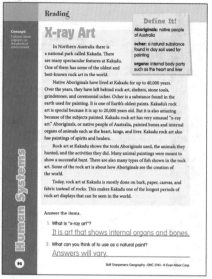

Page 96

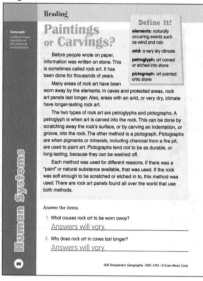

Page 98

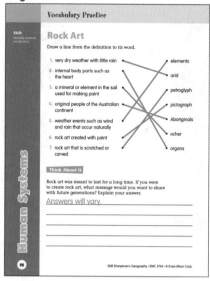

Page 100

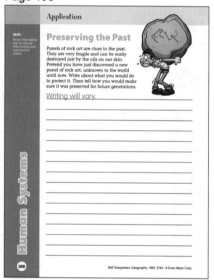

Page 102

Page 104

Page 106

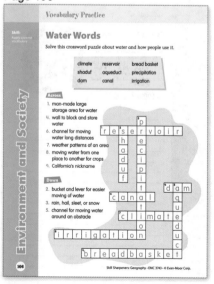

Page 108

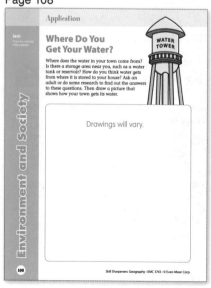

Page 110

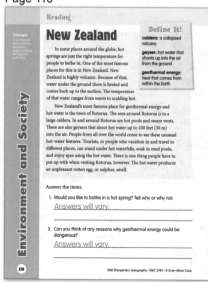

Heat from the Ground

Reading

Concept: The location of an environment provides opportunities for human activities.

Most places in the world get their electricity from fossil fuels. Fossil fuels are coal, oil, and gas. These fuels are not renewable, which means they will run out at some point. Using fossil fuels also causes pollution. Iceland does not use fossil fuels to produce most of their energy. Instead, most homes and businesses in Iceland use geothermal energy to heat their homes, get hot water, and generate, or make, electricity.

Iceland sits directly over a rift, or crack, in Earth's continental plates. That means the plates there are being pulled apart. This causes a large amount of volcanic activity below Iceland's ground. Also, Iceland gets a lot of rain and snow, which trickles underground and heats up.

In the early 1900s, the first Icelander learned how to use this energy to tap into the hot water. Now the government of Iceland has a whole system in place to use geothermal energy and deliver it to its people. There are five main geothermal energy plants in Iceland that do exactly that. Other countries are trying to learn from Iceland in order to use geothermal energy wherever they can, as well.

Define It!

fossil fuels: oil, coal, and gas used for heat and electricity

pollution: land, water, or air that is dirty or harmed

continental plates: huge slabs of rock that float on Earth's surface

Answer the item.

Do you think it is a good idea to use geothermal energy instead of fossil fuels? Explain why or why not.

Answers will vary.

Environment and Society

Amazing Earth

Vocabulary Practice

Skill: Apply geography concepts

Earth is an amazing place that provides many sights to see, resources to use, and natural places to enjoy. Read the description and write the word it describes.

| caldera | geyser | tourists | geothermal |
| fossil fuels | hot spring | rift | continental plates |

1. people who travel to different places — tourists
2. hot water that shoots out of the ground — geyser
3. oil, gas, and coal used for energy — fossil fuels
4. a crack or split in the ground — rift
5. a volcano that has collapsed — caldera
6. huge slabs of rock that float on Earth's surface — continental plates
7. heat that comes from inside Earth — geothermal
8. hot water that comes from underground — hot spring

Think About It

Would you rather see a caldera or a geyser? Tell why.

Answers will vary.

Environment and Society

You Found a Hot Spring!

Application

Skill: Write narrative text about real-world situations

Pretend you just discovered the most amazing hot spring. Thousands of people will want to come and sit in the healing waters, but the hot spring is hard to get to.

Write to tell how you would change the environment to make it ready for people to visit.

- What will you do to the environment around the hot spring so that people can come and enjoy it?
- Where will they stay after they get there?
- Will there be a place for them to buy food or a drink?

Writing will vary.

Environment and Society

Finding Gold

Reading

Concept: The location of resources affects patterns of settlement and trade.

There are several ways miners get gold out of the ground. The most popular way is probably panning. A person sifts through dirt, soil, and rocks in a pan until the heavier gold settles to the bottom of the pan. Finding gold this way can take a long time. Another way to mine for gold is to use a rocker box, also known as a cradle. Using a wooden box, a person sifts through dirt and sand with a strainer that is at the bottom of the cradle. This is called cradling. The dirt and sediment sifts through but the gold is left behind.

To find gold in a very large area of land, miners used to use hydraulic mining. On hillsides where gold was likely to be found, miners used high-powered water cannons to spray down into the soil. The gravel loosened by this was washed through sieves. There, the heavy gold settled and was left behind while the rest of the dirt washed away. However, hydraulic mining was banned over one hundred years ago because the process hurt the environment.

Define It!

panning: using a pan with water to sift through dirt, soil, and rocks to find gold

hydraulic mining: spraying a high-powered hose or hillside to loosen dirt to help find gold

sieves: containers with lots of small holes, used for separating large pieces from small pieces

Answer the items.

1. If you were to try to find gold, would you use a pan or a rocker box? Explain your answer.
   Answers will vary.

2. Which method do you think is best for finding the most gold?
   Answers will vary.

Environment and Society

Australian Gold

Reading

Concept: The location of resources affects patterns of settlement and trade.

One famous area for finding gold is the country of Australia. In 1851, the first grain of gold was discovered near the city of Bathurst. Soon, the area was renamed Ophir. Ophir is a city mentioned in the Bible that was known for its wealth. Within four months, over 1,000 prospectors came there to try to strike it rich. Gold fever then spread across Australia, and miners rushed to the diggings.

Gold was also found in many other areas in Australia. In the state of New South Wales, over 26 metric tons (57,320 pounds) of gold was found in 1852 alone. The neighboring state of Victoria found even more gold than that. Soon, hundreds of thousands of immigrants arrived in the country to mine the goldfields. During the 1850s, the state of Victoria alone produced more than one third of the gold mined elsewhere in the world. Gold was found in even more parts of the country.

Businesses boomed in towns wherever the miners were. Many hotels, restaurants, and telegraphs were built. People made a lot of money because of the miners. Different ways to ship gold from Australia to faraway places such as London were also developed.

Define It!

Ophir: a biblical city known for its wealth

prospector: a person who comes to an area to mine for gold or other minerals

telegraph: lines set up for communication

Answer the item.

Why was a part of Australia named Ophir?

Ophir is a city from the Bible that had a lot of wealth. All the gold found near Bathurst made that city very wealthy, so they renamed it Ophir.

Environment and Society

The Rush for Gold

Vocabulary Practice

Skill: Use visual discrimination

Find these Gold Rush words in the word search.
Hint: Some are backwards.

| australia | ophir | victoria | panning |
| cradling | hydraulic | miners | gold |

Environment and Society

Gold Is Special!

Application

Skill: Write narrative text about real-world situations

Pretend you found a huge gold nugget. What would you do with it? Would you turn it in for money? Would you have it made into a piece of jewelry? Write to tell about it.

Writing will vary.

Environment and Society

Lewis and Clark

Reading

Concept: Historical events are influenced by geographic context.

In 1803, the United States purchased a large piece of land from the French. This land stretched approximately 828,000 square miles (2,144,510 square kilometers) from the Mississippi River all the way to the Rocky Mountains. The land deal was called the Louisiana Purchase. President Jefferson arranged for a group of about 50 men to explore this large area of land and beyond. The group of army volunteers was led by Meriwether Lewis and William Clark. It has since been called the Lewis and Clark Expedition.

Along the way, the group encountered many Native Americans. They befriended one named Sacagawea. She came along with the group to help interpret native languages and calm native groups that may be unfriendly to the explorers.

The Lewis and Clark Expedition had several goals. One was to explore and map the new territory. Another was to find an easy-to-follow, safe route across the country. They also wanted to help establish an American presence in the land before other countries tried to claim it, or take ownership of it. Finally, the Lewis and Clark Expedition studied the plants, animals, and geography of the area.

The journey from St. Louis, Missouri, to the Pacific Ocean and back took two years, four months, and ten days and lasted from May 1804 to September 1806. When the group finally reached the ocean (where Fort Clatsop, Oregon, is now), Lewis called out, "Ocean in view!"

Define It!

Louisiana Purchase: a land deal between the United States and France, in which the U.S. acquired the land west of the Mississippi River

route: places to travel along from one place to another

geography: the natural features of a place, such as rivers and mountains

Answer the item.

What would you have yelled when you saw the ocean?

Answers will vary.

The Uses of Geography

A 1,000-Mile Walk

Reading

Concept: Historical events are influenced by geographic context.

John Muir was a famous conservationist. Muir was well known for helping to protect many areas in the United States, including Yosemite National Park in California.

In 1867 at 28 years old, Muir was nearly blinded by an accident in a factory. When his eyesight returned, he devoted his life to studying the natural world.

Shortly after the accident, 29-year-old Muir began a 1,000-mile walk. He journeyed from Indiana to Florida, taking him nearly two years. In Muir's words, he had no certain route or path to take. But he wanted to go on the "wildest, leafiest, and least trodden way I could find." Muir made the journey alone as much as possible.

There were many days Muir went with little food. He also slept nights without blankets. But Muir said he wandered mile after mile as free as the wind. The walk took him through forests, along streams, and next to bogs. The whole time, Muir basked in the beauty of the land. And that journey helped shape the rest of his life.

Define It!

conservationist: a person who helps preserve and protect the natural world

trodden: walked on

bog: an area of swampy water

Answer the item.

Describe what you think Muir's walk was like.

Answers will vary.

The Uses of Geography

Page 130

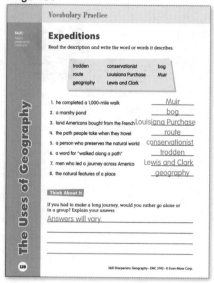

Vocabulary Practice

Skill:
Apply geography concepts

Expeditions

Read the description and write the word or words it describes.

trodden	conservationist	bog
route	Louisiana Purchase	Muir
geography	Lewis and Clark	

1. he completed a 1,000-mile walk _____ Muir
2. a marshy pond _____ bog
3. land Americans bought from the French _____ Louisiana Purchase
4. the path people take when they travel _____ route
5. a person who preserves the natural world _____ conservationist
6. a word for "walked along a path" _____ trodden
7. men who led a journey across America _____ Lewis and Clark
8. the natural features of a place _____ geography

Think About It

If you had to make a long journey, would you rather go alone or in a group? Explain your answer.

Answers will vary.

The Uses of Geography

130

Skill Sharpeners: Geography • EMC 3743 • © Evan-Moor Corp.

Page 131

Hands-on Activity

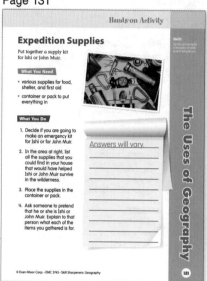

Expedition Supplies

Put together a supply kit for Ishi or John Muir.

What You Need

• various supplies for food, shelter, and first aid
• container or pack to put everything in

What You Do

1. Decide if you are going to make an emergency kit for Ishi or for John Muir.

2. In the area at right, list all the supplies that you could find in your house that would have helped Ishi or John Muir survive in the wilderness.

3. Place the supplies in the container or pack.

4. Ask someone to pretend that he or she is Ishi or John Muir. Explain to that person what each of the items you gathered is for.

Answers will vary.

Skill:
Apply geography concepts in real-world situations

The Uses of Geography

131

© Evan-Moor Corp. • EMC 3743 • Skill Sharpeners: Geography

Page 132

Application

Skill:
Write narrative text about real-world situations

Expedition Journal

There have been many people who have taken long journeys or spent time in the wilderness alone. Pretend that you are one of those people. Write a journal entry that tells where you are, how long you have been there, and what you have seen.

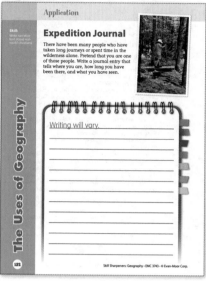

Writing will vary.

The Uses of Geography

132

Skill Sharpeners: Geography • EMC 3743 • © Evan-Moor Corp.
